When Romeo Wrote Juliet

When Romeo Wrote Juliet

Your inspirational guide to the art of writing love letters

BRIAN HOLTCAMP & PAULA HILTON

EDITED BY HARRY GORDON

ILLUSTRATED BY JEFF REED

STYLUS PUBLISHING • SUNNYVALE, CALIFORNIA • 1994

Copyright © 1994 Brian Holtcamp & Paula Hilton. All rights reserved.

No portion of this book may be reproduced or used in any form, or by any means, without prior written permission of the publisher.

Library of Congress Catalog Card Number: 93-94242

When Romeo Wrote Juliet,
Your inspirational guide to the art of writing love letters
by Brian Holtcamp and Paula Hilton

ISBN: 1-884327-17-6

First printed January 1994
Manufactured in the United States of America

The paper used in this book meets the minimum requirements of the American National Standard for Information Services—Permanence of Paper for Printed Library Materials, ANSI Z39.48-1984.

10 9 8 7 6 5 4 3 2 1

Stylus Publishing
P.O. Box 2741
Sunnyvale, CA 94087-0741
(408) 244-6344 Tel
(408) 244-6659 Fax

This book is designed to provide useful information on the subject matter covered. It is sold with the understanding that the publisher and authors are not engaged in rendering professional advice or formal education.

Every effort has been made to make this book as complete and accurate as possible. However, there may be typographical or content mistakes. Therefore, this text should only be used as a general guide.

The purpose of this book is to educate and entertain. The authors and publisher shall have neither liability nor responsibility to any person or entity with respect to any loss or damage caused, or allegedly caused, directly or indirectly by the information contained in this book.

Acknowledgments

*T*HIS BOOK was inspired by many special people. Our thanks go out to all of them for their support and contributions to this effort. In particular, we want to thank the following people:

Publisher: Stylus Publishing

Editor/Designer: Harry Gordon

Illustrator: Jeff Reed

Contributing Romantics: Jim and Valerie Holtcamp
Jim and Polly Hilton

Anne Alexander
Denise Bockwolt
Chris Cole
Alan and Marilyn Dettmering
Diane Gano-Rosete
Char Hill
Keith Kaiser
Colleen Kelsh
Mary Larsen
Joey Leporati

Julie and Brian McNabb
Lisa Ong
Trey and Tiffany Robert
Jamie Sovereign
Megan Stevenson
Dorothy Stevenson
John Surina
Karen Taylor
Cindy Whyte
Peppy Woll

Dedication

To Lynn and Jeff:
Without your love
there could be no love letters

Contents

	Introduction	1
Chapter One	Writing Affectionately	5
Chapter Two	Elements of Passionate Correspondence	13
Chapter Three	Harnessing Inspiration	23
Chapter Four	Styles of Love Letters	41
Chapter Five	Writing Your Letter	61
Chapter Six	Some Real Letters	73
Chapter Seven	Summary and Closing Thoughts	95
Appendix	Tools and Materials	97
	References	115
	Glossary	117

Introduction

> In love there are two things—bodies and words.
>
> —Joyce Carol Oates

*L*OVE IS one of the strongest emotions we are capable of experiencing. It can be powerful, consuming, stimulating, and unforgettable. Whether you're falling in love for the first time or coming up on your golden anniversary, at some point in the relationship you will probably feel an urge to declare your affection in a new way. You may want to express yourself to your loved one in an unforgettable way. Something different. Something timeless. You may not know how to go about doing it, so you may consider sending flowers or going out to dinner at a special place. While there's nothing wrong with flowers or a dinner out, they will not compare to writing a love letter. Once you experience putting your feelings down on paper, you may find you'll never go back to just flowers and dinner again.

There are a number of reasons to write "I love you" on a piece of paper. You may want to express love to a friend or relative. You may want to share passionate feelings with your lover. You may want to remind your husband or wife of the love you feel. Whatever your needs are, be it a stirring, pull-out-the-plugs, lay-it-on-the-line, heart-stopping, one-of-a-kind love letter or a letter expressing affection to a friend or relative, this book will help you. It contains great ideas, helpful hints, and useful information for writing expressive, meaningful, and unforgettable love letters.

The male half of this writing team, Brian, became a believer in the effectiveness of a love letter when he was twenty-one. He was in love with a woman who, from the very beginning of the relationship, pulled him into an unspoken contest as to who could do the nicest thing for the other. After several months of this, he was pleasantly surprised one day when he arrived home and found a love letter from her in the mailbox. They lived only seconds apart (she was his upstairs neighbor) and spent every possible moment together. Yet the fact that she took the time to put her feelings in writing meant more to him than all of the wonderful things she had said or done in the past. Although that relationship ended long ago, he will always be grateful to her for that first love letter because from that point on, he has appreciated the significance of love letters.

Like Brian, Paula's interest in love letters comes from personal experience. Her self-described "true love for all time" began as a simple friendship. The two had worked together briefly, then moved on to new projects at different locations. Because they didn't want the friendship to end, they began corresponding by electronic mail on their home computers. Paula delighted in writing poems and stories for him, while he entertained her with tales about growing up in a large family. After several months of writing, their friendship turned into mutual attraction. They agreed to go out on a dinner date and have been inseparable ever since.

Over the years, Brian and Paula have often discussed love letters with friends and acquaintances, collected examples of

Introduction 3

real love letters from anyone willing to share them, and researched various aspects of letter writing in general. From that experience they have formulated ideas about love letters that should help any struggling, would-be romantic writer. With their combined interest andexperience in writing and receiving love letters, they decided to write this book.

Throughout this book, scenarios using a fictitious, modern Romeo and Juliet are employed to demonstrate how to express yourself sincerely and affectionately. Some scenarios are based on conventional situations; some are not so conventional.

Remember though, this is not a rule book on writing love letters. No such rule book could be taken seriously. There are no formal rules for writing love letters, just as there are no rules for communicating your feelings in any other manner. This book is intended to be used as a guide and was written with the hopes that it will encourage you to put down in writing your feelings for someone you love and make your letter writing fun and unique.

CHAPTER ONE
Writing Affectionately

> In order to create there must be a dynamic force,
> and what force is more potent than love?
>
> —Igor Stravinsky

*P*EOPLE HAVE been showing affection for each other since the beginning of recorded time. The means of expressing that affection has evolved from basic grunting and gesturing to more eloquent forms. The love letter is one of those more eloquent ways of expressing our warm feelings toward another person, and it adds a quality of permanence to that expression.

Aside from talking, writing is the most widely used form of communication. Until the invention of the telephone in 1876, writing was the only way to communicate with someone out of earshot. Modern technology has given us new means to communicate quickly and efficiently, but much of that technology (such as facsimile and electronic mail) depends on the ability to write. While talking is immediate and spontaneous, the written word endures.

Everybody feels passion in one form or another. Not everyone, however, knows how to or feels comfortable expressing that passion, especially in writing. Maybe you have difficulty finding the courage you think you need to write what you feel. Maybe you're afraid of appearing weak or vulnerable. Maybe you feel awkward putting your feelings on paper. Maybe you don't know how to write that "mushy" stuff that love letters seem to call for. Whatever your hesitations, there are many good reasons to pick up a pen and scribe your emotion.

Great Reasons To Write

People are able to communicate via the written word. Writing and speaking are both skills we learn at a young age. We practice our verbal skills almost continuously, but our writing skills are often neglected. If your writing skills have become rusty, they will return quickly with just a few letters.

People love to read good things about themselves. When you are inspired and write affectionately to someone, you can be sure your letter will be reread many times. Sincere, loving words are always welcome!

There are no rules. You can say whatever you want to say, however you want to say it. Your letter is a personal message intended for one person only.

Talk is cheap. Expressing your affection in writing gives it more credibility. Additionally, many people find that they can communicate their feelings with more passion by writing than they can by speaking.

Writing provides a nice alternative to the ordinary events in courtship. Writing is not a substitute for other expressions of affection, but it's a wonderful enhancement. Instead of buying flowers, candy, or cards, write a letter. A letter is more personal than anything you can buy.

You can bypass the normal protocol of romance. You don't have to get dressed up (or even dressed) to write a good love letter. How you look has no relevance. There are no places to be, people to meet, or proper ways to conduct yourself. You don't even have to get out of bed to write!

Gender has no bearing. Whether you are a man or a woman, you can write a great love letter. One sex does not have an advantage over another when writing. You don't need physical strength or a soft touch to write what you feel.

A Real Gift

You and Juliet have been dating for two years. For her 30th birthday, you planned a surprise party at her favorite restaurant. The party was a smashing success, with all of her close friends and family in attendance. When Juliet opened her gifts, you noticed she saved the envelope from you until the very end.

> To My Birthday Girl,
>
> I feel lucky and grateful to be sharing your 30th birthday with you. Since I met you, every day feels like a birthday. You make me feel important — like *I'm* the "birthday boy." You're full of surprises — the anticipation over what's in store for me next is like waiting to open a pile of gifts. You offer me love, warmth, tenderness, and excitement. You make me feel happy, loved, and special.
>
> Today *you're* the birthday girl, and I want you to know how much it means to me to share it

with you. As my gift to you, please accept my invitation to an evening of gourmet delights at my humble abode, complete with candlelight, your favorite music, and a loving me!

All My Love,
Romeo

Despite the party, gifts, and good friends surrounding her on her birthday, the letter from Romeo was the most important part of the evening for Juliet. It was an unexpected declaration from a man who had often said he loved her but had never written the words for her to keep.

For most of us, receiving a personal letter is also a real treat since we can often be too busy to maintain a written dialogue with our friends. Most people we talked with said that the first thing they do every day when they get home is check their mail and sort it, placing anything handwritten in a stack to read later. After tossing out the advertisements and crying over the bills, sitting back and enjoying a warm letter from someone special is a pleasurable way to spend some time.

Writing such a letter is equally pleasurable. It is a wonderful way to share your emotions and passion. Gathering your thoughts, collecting the writing materials, then actually sitting down to create the love letter is an experience that requires time, but it is time well spent.

Your letter can be a simple declaration of love or an elaborate dissertation of your feelings for another. Written confirmation of those feelings will provide your reader with a permanent record that will be enjoyed endlessly.

Philosophy

You and Juliet have been dating for a year. You are a partner in a large law firm, and Juliet is a concert pianist who travels extensively. You are both affluent. On the six month anniversary of your meeting, you deliver the following letter to Juliet:

> Dear Juliet,
>
> I was going to buy you a car in honor of our meeting, but you bought one last week. I thought about giving you a vacation but learned you'll be touring in Europe in just a few months. Your jewelry box resembles a jewelry store, your closet resembles Sak's, and your house was featured in last month's Beautiful Homes. In lieu of a gift you don't need or want, I offer you these written words of love.
>
> Before you, I had become stale and uninspired. I could not see the beauty surrounding me because of the fog enveloping my senses. I was one dimensional, verging on the nondimensional.
>
> Then, you swept into my life like a wave upon a beach. You washed away the footprints of my past and the refuge of my present and smoothed the way for a beautiful future. I am grateful, honored, and still incredulous. Your love was unexpected but not unwelcome. I thank you from the bottom of my heart.
>
>   I Love You,
>   Romeo

Romeo searched his heart for something to give to Juliet that would be meaningful and sincere. He turned on his creative talents and wrote a love note that Juliet treasured. Creativity is an ability everyone is born with, although it still must be developed. Some people are labeled creative because they demonstrate the ability to do something nobody else has done. Everybody can do something new. Creativity is not the exclusive domain of artists, philosophers, and poets.

Some people are predisposed to imaginative thought, but anyone can develop the ability for creative expression. You don't have to limit this expression of affection to someone you are romantically involved with. Your letter may be to a close friend or to a family member. You are writing to express your feelings of fondness and friendship. Those written feelings of love can be shared not only with your lover but also your best friend, teacher, co-worker, or relative.

Expressing love is a natural extension of experiencing love. At a recent 20-year class reunion, a friend was approached by a man who told her he had been in love with her in high school. She had no idea he felt that way about her, and she told him so. He said he had been too shy to let her know then, and he wished he'd had the courage to do something about it at the time. If he had written her a note, however brief, telling her how he felt, his memories of high school might be filled with fun and love instead of loneliness and longing.

There may be someone that you feel close to that you've never told — someone you admire but are hesitant to talk to, maybe even someone you love but are afraid to tell. Take some time to think about your own life, and you may be surprised at the number of people you "owe" a letter to. Use the ideas in this book to help you in this endeavor. Think about all the good reasons to write, and see if you can come up with even one good reason not to.

Your Qualifications

You met Romeo on a blind date six months ago. You seem to have very little in common. You come from different backgrounds, and your professions are as far apart as they can be. You work for the phone company repairing phone lines, and Romeo is a secretary for a temporary agency. Despite all of the differences, you love being together and are already making wedding plans. Romeo is quite the romantic. He writes lengthy love letters to you almost every day during his lunch hour. You enjoy reading the letters, so finally you get up the courage to try writing one of your own.

> *Romeo —*
> *Let me just start out by saying you're better than I am at this. You have the words, I have the moves. I like your words, and I know you like my moves. So far, so good.*
>
> *Now I'll try the words. You are really something. You make me feel good, like I've never felt before. It just seems like everything is better because of you. Not that it was so bad before, but now it's just better.*
>
> *I do want to marry you. I think it will be cool being Mrs. Romeo and Mr. Juliet. I want to be with you. Not just now, but always. I look forward to seeing you and can't imagine a day without you. That's the part that makes everything better. Before I didn't really have anything to*

look forward to and I never imagined anything. I just lived each day without a thought about tomorrow.

I guess that's it, except to say—

*I love you,
Juliet*

Some people are gifted with the ability to make beautiful music, some are eloquent speakers, some paint, and others dance—all to express themselves in ways that others can enjoy. Those are all extensions of natural human abilities. Juliet didn't think she could write a love letter, but she did. She said what she felt and was able to convey those feelings to Romeo. Anybody can write a great love letter.

If you have the basic ability to write in your native language you can develop that ability into an art form as well. Creating something as priceless as a love letter is an art you can learn. We propose that everyone is capable of channeling affection into writing meaningful and passionate letters. The variety in articulating your feelings is limited only by your imagination.

Chapter Two
Elements of Passionate Correspondence

I fall in love with any girl who smells of library paste.

— Charles Schultz (*Peanuts*)

*L*OVE LETTERS have a special significance. They contain very personal thoughts and emotions normally reserved for intimate conversation. Many times these thoughts are never discussed but only written. This style of writing requires a mindset and vocabulary not normally used or even taught in traditional schools. We will explore some writing guidelines (not rules) so your letter truly conveys your affection for the reader.

Normal Evolution of Letter Writing

Anyone who has gone to elementary school has probably been taught how to write a letter. We learned the proper salutations, format, and endings to use and how to address the envelope. Even so, the first letter you wrote was probably written before you learned the proper mechanics of writing. Do you remember the first spontaneous letters you produced in grade school? They were probably the notes you passed to your friends. You would sit in class looking busy and studious while writing intently. Then, when the teacher was not looking, you would fold the note as small as possible and slip it to your friend:

> Juliet
> Please do my spelling list for me tonight. If you will do my spelling list I will stand with you at recess tomorrow and let your friends see me standing with you.
>
> Your friend
> Romeo

Remember your elementary school teacher showing you how to title and format everything?

> Dear Sirs:
> My bot of Sugar Bombs cereal was missing the decoder ring that was promised on the front of the bot. Please mail a ring to the following address.
>
> Sincerely,
> Romeo Brown

From there we graduate to the obligatory letters from school:

Elements of Passionate Correspondence   15

```
Dear Mom and Dad,

School is fine. There's really not much going
on. All I have time to do is study study
study. I'm still planning on coming home over
the 4th. See you then!
                         Love,
                         Juliet



P.S. — Please send money. There's a big beer
bash down at the river next weekend, and I
already spent this month's allotment on
concert tickets and new roller blades.
```

Then we arrive at the office memo we write as adults:

```
R
As per our telecon, manufacturing will
forward you 200 units for distribution for
our west coast office.
                         J
```

As you get older and more affluent, you may eventually have your personal assistant write a letter that starts like this:

```
Dear Sirs,
Your car is a piece of junk. I will never buy
another Ferrari as long as I live…
```

And finally, let us not forget the annual Christmas letter:

Dear Aunt Betty and Uncle Bob,

Merry Christmas! Everything is just fine here. California is as beautiful as ever. We bought a new house this year. It's small and has no yard, but out here you just don't spend that much time at the house. Romeo is doing well at work, despite the fact that he had triple bypass surgery earlier this year and just recovered from double-lung pneumonia. Matt is doing well in school and has finally stopped wetting the bed. Now it seems to be Molly's turn, but we're sure it's just because she has to share her room with the new baby. In another few years we plan on getting another house that's big enough for all of us! We needed a little extra income because of the new house and all, so I've taken up telemarketing. It's fascinating work that I can do at home, plus I get to talk to so many friendly people. Anyway, I hope all is well with you and you have a great Christmas!

Love,
Juliet, Romeo, Matt,
Molly & Melody

When writing a love letter, you are not writing to complain about something or give an update about yourself. You are writing to tell someone how you feel about them. Keep your affection in mind when sitting down to write. Interesting little facts about your location and mindset may lend to the description of your thoughts, but don't go off on a tangent about your broken car or the killing you made in the market.

This will not be true if you are separated from your loved one. You may want to relate day-to-day activities that include thoughts of your love. Reading about how you spent your day will draw your reader closer to you. Thinking about how to word your letter, creating a humorous approach, or planning how to share an office secret can fill your idle time. In turn, your loved one will feel like a big part of your life even though you are not together. This, along with the words of love and longing that naturally come when separated from someone you love, will be cherished.

Golden Opportunity

Love letters are your opportunity to break away from any old biases you may have toward writing. A love letter is a pleasure to write, unlike other types of letters that we write out of a sense of obligation (the thank you note for a well-intentioned but really awful gift) or out of necessity (the letter to the courthouse explaining why the parking ticket is an error because, yes, the license number is yours, but your car is a Toyota, not a Cadillac).

When you are writing a letter, you have the freedom to compose and deliver your thoughts any way you desire. When you are writing a love letter, you have the same freedom, but because it's fun, pleasurable, and exciting, it won't be a chore. Race, religion, age, gender, sexual preference, and nationality have nothing to do with writing a love letter. It's truly an equal opportunity activity.

On a larger scale, nothing in normal, everyday society has anything to do with your letter either. You can write what you feel without regard to anything external. You need not concern yourself with the stock market, the headlines, global warming, or anything else. Just observe some simple guidelines, and let your heart take over.

The Mindset

When writing a love letter, *be sincere.* Write what you feel, not what you think you should feel. False flattery, undue praise, and insincere words of love will be spotted quickly and dismissed by your reader. Conversely, heartfelt prose will be stirring and long remembered. Write what you feel and pass it on. Just writing to a person to say you are thinking of them can be incredibly powerful.

When writing affectionately, *be yourself.* You do not need to emulate someone famous to be well received, although writing like Shakespeare could be fun if you are student of English literature. You can try different writing styles without sacrificing the authenticity of your feelings. But your style should not conceal the affection in your message.

Be inventive and original. Originality occurs as you write because the letter is naturally personalized in several ways. The salutation, the personal articulation of your feelings, and the signature all add originality. The materials you choose (see Appendix A) and your handwriting style also personalize your letter. Since a love letter is directly from your heart to your reader, let your artistic side flourish. Your letter will most certainly be better than any greeting card.

Take time to gather your thoughts. If writing feels like a chore, it will be obvious to your reader. Your letter will reflect your mood, so take the time needed to create the proper mood. Writing your letter may take some time depending on whether you want to scribble a quick note or compose a literary masterpiece. A short love note can take a minute, but a full declaration of heartfelt desire can take hours. Take short breaks to relax if your letter is long.

Have no expectations of your reader. If you write with the purpose of communicating something specific, say what you mean. However, do not expect a certain reaction or you may be disappointed. If you write with a hidden agenda, chances are it will come across loud and clear. Be sincere when you write.

Remain reader oriented as you write. Express your most personal feelings while keeping this special person in the front of your mind. Talk about the many things you admire about the person. Your letter will naturally adopt a gracious tone and please your reader immeasurably.

Mechanics

When possible, hand write your love letter. We realize the many advantages of word processing, but this type of romantic writing is not word processing. Love letters are messages from one heart to another. Therefore, the handwritten document possesses the originality of authorship and the uniqueness of one person's written communication. Laser printed documents are to handwritten letters what a poster of a Van Gogh painting is to the original oil on canvas.

(An exception to that guideline would be for people with disabilities that make it hard or impossible to write with a pen. For those special people, computers and associated input devices designed for the disabled are sometimes the best, if not the only way, to communicate. The Nobel prize winning physicist Stephen Hawking is limited to communicating through a computer with only one button, which he uses to continually astonish humankind with new ideas.)

Be very descriptive. There are innumerable beautiful and original ways to express your thoughts. Vividly imagine the scene or emotion and use vivid adjectives to describe it. Describing emotion is no more difficult than describing physical properties. You can use terms such as *warm, comforting,* or *calming* to convey your feelings. Do not presume your reader knows exactly what you are thinking. Your loved one will delight in reading in print the detailed description of your thoughts. It shows sensitivity to have taken the time to think about what you want to say and how to say it.

Use punctuation such as exclamation points, underline, etc. to highlight important thoughts. Passionate writing requires indicators of your emotion. Underlining important phrases and using all capital letters to say "I LOVE YOU" will make the point unmistakably. Remember though, a little goes a long way. If every sentence ends with "!" it will be hard to distinguish where the really big points are.

Avoid clichés. Even if you really believe her hair looks like spun gold, think of an alternative way to state what you feel. "Every time I look at your hair, I'm reminded of Hawaii and that brilliant golden sunset…" will not only win her heart, but may get you both thinking of a trip to Hawaii! It's fine to use famous quotes and clichés at times, but try not to pepper your prose with overused expressions. Almost anything can be restated creatively with a little thought.

Break thoughts into paragraphs. It is easy to become long winded but you don't have to write every word that comes to mind. Instead, gather your thoughts and write sentences and paragraphs that are digestible. Strive for quality over quantity. The best jazz musicians evolve a style where nuance is their trademark. Often, less is more.

Use vocabulary that you don't use every day. Many people find themselves using the sterile jargon of their particular trade for most of their communication, but the language of love is full of passion and emotion. Show your sensitive side by sprinkling amorous terms in your letter.

Avoid vulgar language unless you know it will be received without incident. If the topic is sex, be sophisticated and use gentle descriptive terms. Although "talking dirty" can be erotic, it is best to be sure your reader will be receptive. Being suggestive via metaphor and innuendo has a much greater impact than simple pornography. Even if the letter is lusty, make it classy!

Keep the tone consistent and avoid sarcasm. Spoken sarcasm can usually be recognized because of voice inflection, but the same words may come across differently when written. Also, a reader can become confused if the mood of your letter changes radically from joy to irritation in one sentence. If you are suddenly feeling cranky, take a break and reflect on your affection. The warm emotions you generate in your reader will escalate endlessly if you are consistent in what you write.

Use metaphor. Never compare someone to an inanimate object such as a car. Chances are some Italian race car designer modeled the body of his car after a female and not vice versa. Pick gentle and organic objects. There is an abundance of beautiful items found in nature.

Stay off the editing treadmill. Whether you are handwriting or composing your letter on a computer, don't get mired in analysis of the format. Neat margins and double spacing between paragraphs are irrelevant to the content of your letter. And don't worry about flaws—flaws are natural and expected in any work of art.

Finally, *be positive when you write.* If you consider what the average person reads on a daily basis, your joyful words will be a welcome change from the mayhem of the newspaper and the bills and solicitations in the mailbox. Make your letter a ray of light beaming into your reader's soul.

Chapter Three
Harnessing Inspiration

> Be still when you have nothing to say;
> when genuine passion moves you,
> say what you've got to say,
> and say it hot.
>
> —D.H. Lawrence

*G*ETTING "in the mood" is necessary for almost any activity you can think of, from shopping for a dress to playing touch football with the guys. If you aren't in the right mood, it's hard to find the energy and enthusiasm to write passionately.

Writing a love letter requires a special mood. Fortunately, you can find the desire to write passionately using some simple techniques to alter your habits. Our ideas should just be the catalyst for generating your own ideas, with one idea leading to another and another. Suddenly you'll find you can hardly wait to put your thoughts down on paper!

Take the time you need to find inspiration. You can start by locating a place where you are comfortable. You can sit at a desk or a kitchen table, go to the park, lie in bed, sit in your car, crawl under your pool table, or go up into the attic. Once you are comfortable and focused, let your imagination go. You'll surprise yourself in addition to surprising the one you love! Find what works for you, but never quit experimenting. Since love is always growing, the experience surrounding love can continue growing as well.

Taking Time to Relax

Your first wedding anniversary is tomorrow. You have been putting in long hours at work and haven't had time to buy a gift or even a card for your husband, Romeo. On every special occasion before this, you've each hidden a small gift under the other's pillow. You're getting ready for bed when suddenly you realize you have nothing to put under his pillow. You remember a song he mentioned he liked and decide to write it down as a gift to him.

> *Romeo, Romeo, I want to be your Juliet.*
>
> *Sorry hon, that's all I could remember. The past year has been the best. Too tired to tango. I'll try again next year.*
>
> *Love,*
> *Juliet*

After writing that "love letter," Juliet reread it several times and decided it didn't contain the message she wanted to convey. She sounded tired and uninspired. She decided to try several ideas she had read about in an excellent book on love letters she'd picked up recently. She made herself a cup of hot tea, went into the living room, put on some quiet music, and thought about the past year with Romeo. After just a few minutes, she felt a rush of emotion and could hardly wait to write again.

> *My Darling Romeo,*
>
> *You are the most wonderful and understanding husband any woman could ever hope for. The past few weeks have been difficult with all the long hours, but you've been there for me, just as you always have been. I love being married to you and know my feelings for you will only grow with time. You are handsome, witty, fun, and sexy, and I'm proud to be your wife.*
>
> *I love you, Romeo, and as the song goes, "I want to be your Juliet."*
>
> *Always,*
> *Juliet*

What did Juliet do right? She decided to do more to get in the mood to write. Sometimes feeling that magic for someone is not inspiration enough. Sometimes the desire to write will just roll over you like a warm Hawaiian wave. Other times it may take something to steer your thoughts in that direction—anything that allows your mind to wander and your thinking to change, as this change of thought is often the creative process at work.

Also, Juliet knew that placing herself in a different location was out of the question, so she decided to change the existing environment. She put on romantic music and lowered the lights. Any deviation from your normal routine can change your mood. Sometimes we get so caught up in routine that taking a different route home from work can be an adventure.

When Romeo looked under his pillow the next morning, he was not disappointed when he found only the letter from Juliet. Her letter meant more to him than anything she'd given him in the past. Those few extra minutes made a real difference!

Think About It First

You and Juliet have been dating each other for several years. You are both in college carrying demanding loads. The relationship has been going well for the most part, but tonight at the library you snap at Juliet over something quite trivial. This launched you into a full-on argument, and Juliet ended up walking back to her dorm in a huff. When you got back to your room, you knew you needed to do something but didn't know what. You spotted a love letter book on your dresser (Juliet gave it to you on Valentine's day) and decided a love letter would do the trick. In between reading History of Germany 302 and composing a short story using a given list of verbs for Composition 101, you wrote to Juliet.

Dear Juliet,

I'm sorry you got upset with me this evening. Of course you know how I feel about you. You're a hoot to hang with. Just put this aside and let's get on with it.

Love,
Romeo

What did Romeo do right? He made an effort by writing a letter to Juliet. When Juliet found the letter the following day stuffed under her door mat at the dorm, she could hardly believe her eyes. It seemed Romeo had actually read that love letter book she had given him! She eagerly opened the envelope and read the note he had written inside. Although it wasn't the outpouring she was hoping for, she appreciated his attempt to express his feelings for her in writing. The disagreement seemed trivial compared to his efforts, and their relationship was enhanced.

What could he have done better? Writing because you feel obligated or guilty about something is usually not a good idea. Romeo was using a love letter as a quick fix to an uncomfortable situation. He needed to be relaxed and romantic. He should have thought about his reasons for desiring to communicate his affection. Often you can find your source of inspiration out of those reasons. Wait for the right time, but remember, the right time may be anytime, so have a pen and paper handy at all times!

Romeo should have assumed the correct state of mind by creating or moving to an environment to make him feel amorous and think about the subject at hand. Rather than writing the letter in between school assignments, he should have written the letter first then finished his assignments. Some people prefer warm and comfortable places. Others like lots of activity. If you are easily distracted, find a quiet place away from people, telephones, or anything else that commands your attention. If you prefer being with others, find a restaurant or coffee shop with a suitable atmosphere, and order a favorite beverage or dish. Experiment until you find what you like. Even if you know exactly what works for you, try something new. Remember the importance of changing your surroundings to stimulate different parts of your creative self.

If Romeo had simply finished his homework then written the letter to Juliet, it might have looked something like this:

> Dear Juliet,
>
> I'm sorry about tonight. I thought about what happened at the library and realized I was being unfair. Things got out of hand and I said things I didn't mean. I take them all back! You are the best part of my life and I couldn't even think about going to class tomorrow if you were still

mad at me. I'll be waiting outside the library at our usual spot at 8:00 a.m. to make up.

*Love,
Romeo*

Seize the Moment

You are a busy account executive at a large company, and the demands on your time are endless. Despite this, you met a woman six months ago who is always on your mind. Juliet is incredible, and even though you think about her more than you're with her, she seems to understand, and your time together is always enjoyable. Last night was particularly memorable, and you are having a difficult time concentrating during a meeting you're supposedly chairing.

Ten minutes into the meeting you excuse yourself, saying you need to pick up some notes you left on your desk. You close the door, jot down what you're thinking, seal the note up and send it (via courier) to where she works. Back at your meeting, you are able to concentrate on the task at hand, only smiling once or twice when remembering what you had written.

Incredible Juliet,

*How can a man sit in a meeting
when her glance, however fleeting,
is all he can recall?*

*How can a man, during discussion,
think clearly, without repercussion,
when he's climbing up the wall?*

How can a man go over reports
when her tender moist retorts
is all that makes him fall?

How can a man give full attention
when her name cannot be mentioned
without him running down the hall?

I can hardly wait until Next Tuesday—

Romeo

What did Romeo do right? Most important, he was in the mood to write and he did. If you are in the mood to write, do it. Don't put it off until later and think you will be able to recall the inspiration on demand. It rarely works for anybody. The ideas and thoughts may linger, but recalling the emotion is difficult, and the thoughts will quickly fade.

Even though Romeo was in the middle of something important, he figured out a way to put his feelings down on paper. If it is inconvenient to write because you are in a meeting (where you are supposed to be paying attention) or you are driving, improvise. Have a notepad ready and scribble down whatever you can. Make up an excuse to get away for a few minutes. You'll be surprised at how quickly you can get your thoughts down when you're inspired. If you're in a car, you could use a microcassette recorder to tape your thoughts and write them down later.

There is no substitute for true emotional inspiration when it comes to writing. The passion you feel for another can be channeled into some wonderful prose if you are in the mood to write. Take advantage of those fits of desire to permanently record your feelings.

Harnessing Inspiration

Everything Else Can Wait

You are a busy account executive at a large company, and the demands on your time are endless. Despite this, you met a man six months ago who is always on your mind. Romeo is incredible, and you want to let him know how you're feeling. You schedule a full Saturday morning to do nothing but compose a love letter to Romeo that will set his heart on fire.

When Saturday morning arrives, your phone starts ringing before you can even open your eyes. After three phone calls, you decide enough is enough. This was time scheduled to write your love letter. You know that if you don't use your time wisely, it will be weeks before you can try again. So, you unplug the phone. Next, since you aren't feeling particularly romantic, you put on Romeo's robe ("accidentally on purpose" left at your place), light a fire in the fireplace, turn the stereo on low, take out a photo album filled with pictures of the two of you, and sit down to sip a cup of almond-flavored coffee (Romeo's favorite). Soon you feel inspired to compose that heart-thumping letter you'd envisioned.

> *Oh Romeo,*
>
> *The past six months have been so delicious, so incredible, so fabulous, I can't let another day pass without telling you what it all means to me. You are, without a doubt, the most fantastic man I've ever known. How one man can be gorgeous, sexy, funny, sexy, smart, sexy — did I say sexy? You are one helluva sexy man.*
>
> *I think I've fallen madly head-over-heels in love with you... no, I <u>know</u> I've fallen madly head-over-heels in love with you. How can one woman be so lucky, to be in love with you?*

> *It must be destiny. I'm sitting here, in your warm robe, looking at a picture of your gorgeous face, and I know I'll never get enough of you.*
>
> <u>*I can hardly wait until next Tuesday.*</u>
>
> *Love,*
Juliet

What did Juliet do right? She knew she needed to do something to get in the mood, so she began by putting on his robe. A loved one's belongings can be a powerful source of inspiration.

If you are married or have been dating awhile, you may have acquired some of your lover's personal belongings. If not, swipe a few! Nothing too valuable or anything that would be missed, of course — just something that reminds you of him or her. Any item that stimulates one of your senses will jog memories: a letter, a piece of jewelry, or maybe a nightshirt with your lover's scent. The sense of smell has been documented as one of the most powerful when it comes to activating the memory. You may also leave some reminders of your presence with them. (This may help preclude any kleptomaniac tendencies and accusations of missing underwear between you and your lover.)

Look at a photograph of your loved one. When Juliet took out her album filled with pictures of the two of them, those pictures triggered incredible feelings of love. Some say "a picture is worth a thousand words." If the photo is of someone you care deeply for, you may have more than a thousand words to say.

Choose a picture that reminds you of a wonderful time you had together — the most fun you ever had together or the closest you ever felt to that person.

Listen to music and use it to stimulate your creativity. Think carefully about what you want to convey, and listen to some appropriate music. You might try writing as if your words were going to be put to music. You do this by listening to a favorite piece of music and composing your own lyrics. Instrumental music such as classical, new age, or jazz may be best. Give the music a good listen and let your mind wander.

Write Out of Left Field

You and Juliet have been dating for some time. You are slightly "different" from other people. You've never been a conformer. You're intelligent, witty, fun, and slightly crazy. You're easy to recognize — you're the guy carrying the water pistol in the library. When you decided to write Juliet a love letter, you didn't want it to read like any other love letter she'd ever received. You wanted this love letter to be remembered for all time! Juliet has a cat that she just loves, so after watching Juliet and her cat for a couple of days, you go out into her backyard, climb a tree, and write down your thoughts.

> Dear Juliet,
>
> I love this tree. Because when I'm in this tree I can see you in the kitchen. Sometimes you're baking bread. Sometimes you're doing the dishes. Sometimes you're putting my food in a bowl for me. I just like looking at you, no matter what you're doing.

I was just remembering this morning when I walked down the hall. You were at the end of the hall, and I had to stop for a second just to look at you. You had just gotten up, and with your hair all messy like that it reminded me of the time we chased each other up and down the house. You were laughing and throwing pillows at me. I was laughing and jumping out at you every chance I got. Your hair was all messy that time too.

You sure do look pretty in the mornings. You actually look pretty all the time. I sometimes wish I were Romeo because he gets to do a lot more than just look at you. You sure do know how to make a cat feel good. I'll never run away because of you and this tree.

Love,

What did Romeo do right? To begin with, he wrote a letter that was right coming from him. A traditional letter would have been out of character. Think about who you are when you sit down to write, and the letter will come from your heart.

He used his imagination. You might try imagining yourself as Ernest Hemingway sitting in front of a big fire with a fountain pen in hand. This just might inspire a literary work of art. Remember, great writers use the same tools that are available to you: pen, paper, and inspiration.

He put himself in a different environment (the tree). This is a fantastic way to begin the creative process. Move yourself out of your element. Look for an environment that will allow you to think and compose your thoughts. This can be any place you find comfortable. Visit a neighboring town, take a bubble bath, climb to a grassy knoll overlooking a lake, or find an empty office on the noon hour.

Allow the location to have a profound impact on your inspiration. Moving about to different locations not only is inspirational but can also change your mood. Familiar places can bring back memories. Being in a place where you shared company will remind you of the feelings you had, while new places will give you fresh thoughts. Some places are more sensual than others. Seek out such places if your subject matter requires that kind of inspiration.

He remembered an event that was shared. This can be enough to trigger the creative process. This could be a significant event or something as simple as a drive to work together. You may find that thinking about events you've shared inspires you to write about them. In doing so, the length of time you have known someone is not as important as the ability to recall the events.

draped around her shoulders, and pulled her slowly toward him until he was able to gently kiss her.

When my grandmother told me this story, my eyes filled with tears over the romantic, loving images she described. I was reminded of our first meeting and of our first kiss several months later. Like my grandmother, I'll never forget that kiss, when you pulled me close in the rain, reached down to dry my face with your handkerchief, then kissed me softly. The warmth of your breath, the look in your eyes, the smell of the rain — those images will remain with me forever.

Words alone cannot possibly express how deeply I love you and how happy I am to have been your wife for the past 25 years. You have been a wonderful husband, father, and friend, and I cherish every moment we have spent together.

I love you with all my heart and soul,
Juliet

What did Juliet do right? Juliet used a social gathering as a means of finding inspiration. Most people have a couple of good stories about past or current loves, and often those stories will help you to recall your own experiences and feelings.

Juliet went to her grandmother as a source of romance. Older people are wonderful sources of interesting stories. There is no substitute for experience. Get them to talk about the past. Many older people have led very rich lives and have a supply of wonderful stories to tell. If you want to get some great ideas for how true romance is conducted, talk to someone a generation or two ahead or yours. You will not only be surprised at how things have changed but also by the number of things that have not.

Ask if they have any old love letters they will let you read. Chances are much of their romantic communication took place on paper. They did not have the "benefit" of telephones and data processing equipment. They had to wait for the mailman to bring news from their lover, and those letters can be a wonderful source of inspiration.

When the Goin' Gets Tough

You are a hopeless romantic. You secretly read romance novels along with the classics, your favorite movie is *An Affair to Remember,* and you model yourself after Cary Grant, your all-time favorite movie star. You don't just **become** a romantic when you're romantically involved, you **are** a romantic all the time. When Juliet moved into the office two doors down, you were immediately smitten and did everything in your power to get her to go out with you. Juliet wasn't impressed and declined your invitations. After several weeks with still no date, Juliet arrived in her office one morning and found a note from you.

> *Juliet,*
>
> *Although we barely know one another, I must tell you how I feel. I feel like a mountain climber who is just ten yards from the mountain top he's strained for weeks to reach... like the*

downhill skier standing at the top of the run, about to ski down for the first time all winter... like a hang-glider pilot, harnessed to his glider and standing on the bluff, ready to make the leap... like an ice-skater, skating around the ring in front of thousands of spectators, just seconds before he attempts his first triple... like a diver standing at the edge of the diving board.

Need I say more? The past few weeks, I've been waiting in breathless anticipation for you to say "yes." "Yes" to a night out with me, a night to talk and laugh and enjoy each others' company for the very first time.

Please grant me that first "yes." How about dinner tonight?

Sincerely,
Romeo

What did Romeo do right? He wrote a thoughtful, sincere, and insightful letter. Juliet was surprised and taken aback by this letter. It wasn't at all what she expected. She decided on the spot to give Romeo a try and went right down to his office to deliver the "yes" he'd been waiting for.

Since Romeo is a hopeless romantic, his whole life is ripe for writing sincere love letters. He reads the masterpieces of literature that focus on romance, and he also finds good examples in modern romance novels. In the process, he discovers new and interesting ways to phrase ideas and finds new words to use in his letters.

Romeo also watches romantic movies. Several people told us they had their own favorite romantic comedy they could watch over and over. When they wanted to feel romantic, they'd pop in the video and watch it. Examples cited over and over again were *When Harry Met Sally, What's Up Doc?, Starting Over, Working Girl,* and *The Goodbye Girl.* (We don't recommend *Casablanca* or *Gone With the Wind* for getting in the mood to write a love letter to a current love!)

You will notice an improvement in your love letters as you expose yourself to more material that pertains to the subject of love. Of course the most improvement will come from actually writing, not just reading.

Chapter Four
Styles of Love Letters

> The difference between the right word
> and the almost right word is the difference
> between lightning and a lightning bug.
>
> — Mark Twain

WHEN YOU sit down to write a love letter, it helps to know what your intentions are. Ask yourself: Is this a declaration of love or a reinforcement of love that has already been acknowledged? Your first "I love you" or an "I love you" that has spanned 30 years or more? Someone you've known only briefly or someone you've spent the better part of your life with? Are you declaring love or lust? Do you already feel close to this person, or are you hoping for a closeness to come? Have you been companions but now you want more? Is this a love that has not been returned? Are you desperate to resolve an emotional crisis?

If you have a special message, the focus of your writing will be clear. You can write with a distinctive tone toward a specific ending when you know what you want to say. However, there are many instances where there is no goal. Maybe you simply need to vent your passion and this is the only outlet.

The tone of your love letter will depend on your intent in writing. If you want your reader to feel a warm glow, breathless anticipation, hot longing, or that warm fuzzy feeling, you will use words and phrases to evoke that feeling.

Love Note

You got up 20 minutes late this morning and are rushing around like a maniac to get ready for work. You look over at your sleeping lover and feel that familiar rush of joy at your being together. You don't have time to write a full-fledged love letter, but you can't let this moment pass without some tangible evidence.

> Dear Juliet,
>
> If every morning were as harried as this, it would still be OK because you are in my life. I can hardly wait until tonight!
>
> Love, love,
> and more love
> Romeo

A love note is short and sweet. Just write what is on your mind and leave it for your lover. The love note will typically look hurried since it is designed to communicate immediately. There is no time for a wax seal or calligraphy here. Just jot it down and deliver it. This type of a warm message will be well received when your lover is busy with a normal day's events. Finding it in a briefcase or purse will be like getting a Christmas present early.

Do not discount love notes as childish, silly, or insignificant. Just the indication that you were thinking of your reader is very important. Keep a notepad and pen handy for your love notes.

Some romantics have done things like writing "I love you" on a car or bathroom mirror using bar soap or lipstick. A covert way would be to write it on a bathroom mirror with your finger. The only time it will be visible is when the bathroom steams up. Another extreme for writing short notes is using a children's colored liquid soap called "Zoo Goo." It comes in a little tube like toothpaste and you can squeeze it out onto your partner to draw or write messages. The inspiration you feel when you write on your lover's body in the tub can be very stimulating.

Another way to create an interesting love note would be to cut out a comic strip or article you think your lover would enjoy and attach a note briefly explaining why it made you think of them.

Try leaving your message like lovers of past generations: carve it into a park bench or wet cement. We're not encouraging you to deface public property, but sometimes these things are already started for you. Have you ever been in a restaurant where there were all sorts of things written on the walls and ceilings showing affection of one person for another?

You don't need a volume of material to write a nice little note sharing a passing thought. Random thoughts often occur when you are doing things like walking the dog or taking a shower. If these thoughts happen to be on the subject of romance, write them down when it's convenient and send them off. This is a nice way to share your feelings, a little at a time. A continuous flow of small letters is sometimes better than waiting to compile enough thoughts for an epic. This is also a good way to stay in practice for writing. Soon your vocabulary will increase and your grammar will improve.

One final item about love notes. By definition notes are short. The contents may be a sentence or two to make plans, say thank you, or pay a compliment. This may also be a good way to start writing love letters. You can test the waters with a few short love notes, then later move on to full-blown impassioned declarations of desire.

I Love You

You met Romeo six months ago at a friend's birthday party. You started dating on a casual basis, but somewhere along the line you found yourself very much in love with the guy. You spend most of your time with him, have hinted at how you feel, but haven't openly admitted your feelings. What should you do?

> *Dear Romeo,*
>
> *Several years ago I was hiking in Colorado when I came upon a doe standing beneath a tree. She was frozen in place, gazing off in the distance. I must have stood there for five minutes staring at that doe. I just kept thinking how beautiful she was, and how I would probably never see a more breathtaking sight in my life.*
>
> *Suddenly a buck came out of the trees to stand beside her, and I was filled with awe at the majestic sight before me. I*

was struck by the completeness of the picture before me, and how, just moments before, I believed that picture could not be improved upon.

My life seems to have taken on that same form. I was happy and content. I saw beauty, felt wonder, and experienced joy. I thought my picture was complete.

Then, like that buck, you came out of nowhere and completed my picture. Beauty, wonder, and joy have been intensified by your presence, and the element of love is no longer missing.

I love you.
Juliet

When you decide to declare your love to someone, be it the first time or the one-hundredth time, an "I love you" says it all. It is a powerful phrase that evokes feelings of happiness, joy, and excitement.

The first "I love you" is monumental. Do you remember the first time you said those three words? How nervous you were, how it seemed like you just couldn't breathe until you said it. If you were out on a date, didn't it seem like the night dragged on and on, while you waited for the exact moment to casually slip in that very first, very special "I love you"?

The written "I love you" is equally as important. You aren't just saying "I love you." You're saying "I love you — not only when we're together, but when we're not!" You're telling that special someone that it's a love worth writing about.

Thank you

You have known Juliet for over twenty years. When you started college many years ago, your math class was incredibly difficult so you decided to find a tutor. You saw Juliet's name on a bulletin board offering tutoring and you phoned her. She was a big help, and over the next four years she was always available whenever you called. You know you couldn't have gotten through all of the math and become a rocket scientist if it weren't for Juliet, and now she's tutoring your daughter! Isn't it time you told her how much her help meant?

Juliet,

Someone like you doesn't come around very often, and I feel incredibly fortunate that you came into my life when you did. You not only helped me through my math classes, but you taught me how to persevere. You showed me that with the right attitude and a little effort, I could succeed where before I would have failed. I appreciate everything you did for me, and I thank my lucky stars my daughter is fortunate enough to have your help as well.

Thank you from the bottom of my heart!
Romeo

People often think to *say* "thank you," but a *written* "thank you" means so much more. One woman we spoke with said she sent such a thank you note to her daughter's dance teacher. The dance teacher had a reputation for being tough, but the children who came up through her classes not only could dance the socks off their competition, they also all showed unusual responsibility and organization for kids their age.

Why? Because to dance with that teacher, you had to be responsible and organized. This mother recognized that and sent off a letter. The next time the dance teacher saw this mother, she thanked the mother and said, "People rarely take the time to write those kinds of things down anymore. I really appreciate the fact that you did."

Companionship

You've been friends with Juliet forever. You met in the third grade, and you wrote your first love letter to her:

> Juliet
> i love you
> do you love me?
> yes   no   maybe
>   Romeo

Over the years that puppy love turned to friendship, and lately you've found yourself turning to Juliet for advice and companionship that you haven't been able to find with anyone else. How do you tell her how special she is?

> *My dear friend Juliet,*
>
> *I haven't stopped often enough just to tell you how special you are. Our friendship means more to me than anything. With you, I am constantly reminded of the value of warm companionship. I will always be your friend.*
>
> *Love*
> *Romeo*

Notes thankful of friendship fall into the category of love letters because the two emotions, love and friendship, are often related. These letters may take more courage to write because society has taught us to be "cool." This usually translates to appearing strong, like you really do not need anybody or anything else. This may be true, but good friendship is valuable and no close friend would ever think ill of you for sending a letter expressing that person's importance to you.

Letters to friends will not be about passion and desire. However, they will be similar to love letters because of the feelings of trust, reliability, and fondness associated with friendship. Some people believe that the only things you take with you after this life are the feelings and memories of your relationships with other people. We have read of many instances where a person's last words are a desire to be remembered as a good friend, husband, wife, mother, or father.

When you are writing to a friend, revive the memories that make you feel strongly about that person. Discuss the memories and the feelings in a way relevant to your reader. This will be well received. Few people take the time to talk about their friendship, let alone write about it.

You don't need a special occasion to send a letter to a friend, but you may send one after an event you have been included in such as a party or wedding. Sending a note to say you are thinking of them is OK anytime.

Companionship Turned to Love

You and Juliet have been friends since childhood. You've been spending all of your free time together since you both recently ended relationships you were involved in. You both loved "When Harry Met Sally" but never thought it could happen to you. Then suddenly you realize your feelings have changed to more than just friendship. Companionship is no longer enough.

My Dearest Juliet,

I haven't stopped often enough just to tell you how special you are. Our friendship means more to me than anything, and I never want to do anything to jeopardize that friendship. But I must tell you that my feelings for you have deepened in the past few months, and I can't keep these feelings to myself any longer. I want our relationship to grow from "just friends" to something more. I hope you will give this a chance. How about dinner and a movie tonight? (How does "When Harry Met Sally" sound?)

*Love,
Romeo*

This type of situation can be difficult. It usually catches the people involved completely off guard. They weren't looking for love. They were just friends who spent a lot of time together. They've known each other forever. Maybe they even disliked each other when they first met. Then suddenly they're thrust into this new situation. It usually starts as an awareness of each other. Soon you are looking forward to seeing each other, talking on the phone, relating a story to the other, and sharing life's day-to-day events.

Next comes the attraction, the physical excitement of being near each other. At that point you start asking yourself what's going on, or maybe you try to deny that anything is going on at all. But before you know it, you're not "just friends" anymore and something has to be done.

A love letter is an excellent way to segue into this new relationship. You're taking control of the situation in a positive way. You're admitting to new feelings for this person, and you're showing your sincerity by writing about it. Write in whatever style seems appropriate to you—passionately, logically, with humor, with humility—however you feel comfortable.

By writing down your feelings and delivering the message, you give the other person a chance to read the letter, react to the news (if it is news), and think about the situation—all with complete privacy. No one is put on the spot or made to feel embarrassed. If the feelings are returned, the relationship has a good chance to continue. If not, it's easier for both to deal with the situation when you've both been given a chance to think about what's going on and what to do about it. As difficult as this situation can be, a well-thought-out love letter can ease the difficulty.

Impassioned Declaration

You and Juliet have been seeing each other for two weeks now. From the first meeting, it was obvious you were perfect for each other. You spend every waking moment together, are on the phone constantly, and have planned dates with each other all the way up until the year 3000. The problem is, you haven't yet verbalized those feelings, and the anticipation is killing you!

> *My Darling Juliet,*
>
> *If I don't tell you soon, I'm going to burst. I never in my wildest dreams thought this would happen to me. I planned on a nice long bachelorhood with all the trimmings. I planned on becoming successful, wealthy, powerful, and older before settling down. But since I met you, those plans have been thrown right out the window. I love you madly and want nothing other than to spend my life with you. And I'm ready to start NOW!*
>
> *Romeo*

This is what many people have in mind when they imagine a love letter. This is the total been-womped-upside-the-head-with-love, bare-the-innermost-elements-of-your-soul, hold-absolutely-nothing-back letter. You will be truly inspired when you sit down to write this one. This letter is noncerebral, entirely heartfelt. The emotion will pour from your pen onto the paper as you express your passion in such a way that there will be absolutely no doubt in your reader's mind as to what you feel.

The whole experience of writing an impassioned declaration has a very natural feel to it. Although we have discussed harnessing inspiration, this emotion is the type that just arrives by itself and usually cannot be summoned. It may come from a significant event such as first discovering you are in love. It may also come from a feeling of desperation such as the threat of losing love. Maybe it is the first "morning after" and you still feel that lingering rapture.

Whenever you feel this rush of inspiration, get it down on paper, seal it up, and send it off. Do not proof it, not even for misspellings. If you proof the letter an hour later when the inspiration has subsided, you will probably tone it down to appear "intelligent" or otherwise professional. Don't ruin it!

You may find that you enjoy this style of writing the most. It is quite a rush to vent intense emotion with words. You never seem to experience a shortage of things to say. You can generate volumes when you feel this passionate about your subject. There is no substitute for enthusiasm.

If you are inclined to write spontaneous letters, it will help to have a collection of good writing materials readily available. A few sheets of paper and a pen will do. However, you may just want to scribble thoughts down in what appears to be (truthfully so) a hurried state. This will reinforce the urgency of your message to your reader. Just try not to procrastinate when you feel the inspiration because you never know when it will return.

Novella

You and Juliet live a storybook life together. You love her madly and still can't believe you're together. She knows how you feel, and to your surprise she feels the same way. Because you enjoy making her laugh, the love letters you write to her often take on an amusing style.

> Once upon a time, there was a girl engineer and a boy engineer who lived in the beautiful brown hills of California in different houses in different towns. One day the girl engineer came running around a corner at work with an armload of books and ran smack-dab into the boy engineer. The girl engineer was a volleyball player in her spare time so was no little tiny petite thing that could do no damage but a great big tall woman with strong legs and arms who could easily knock several boy engineers down at once if she wanted to.
>
> In this case she just knocked down the one, and when he came to he looked up and saw the most beautiful woman he had ever seen. She had huge brown eyes, tanned skin, and long straight

blonde hair. He thought he must be dreaming, and he thought he better quit breathing because he didn't want the dream to end.

The girl engineer saw the boy engineer turning blue and decided he must need artificial respiration. She (having been trained in CPR) began administering this life-saving technique to the boy and was quite surprised to find she was being kissed! She pulled away, took one look into his big brown eyes, and decided kissing was definitely better than breathing anyway. They proceeded to kiss in the hall until the manager came to see what the fuss was about (there was quite a crowd around them at this point).

He broke up the encounter but didn't break up the romance. The boy and girl no longer live in different houses in different towns in the brown hills of California. They live in the same house in the same town, and boy are they happy.

*All my love Juliet,
from your Romeo!*

A novella is another term for a short story. When people are in love, they think of each other often. These thoughts and fantasies are the material for a great novella. This is more of a project than a love note, but if you have the time and a desire to voice your imagination, the results can be magnificent.

Imagine your reader receiving your story in the mail. It will be twice as interesting if you use your reader and yourself as the main characters. The possibilities for subject matter are endless. You may write a fairy tale with kings, queens, and knights or an adventure in an animal-filled jungle. (You may include yourself in the cast as anything you like.) Try writing about your lover as if you were her pet fish and were observing her all day. Write favorably though. Don't use this letter to say your aquarium needs cleaning. Try a steamy love fantasy or a science fiction story complete with an alien landscape where you…

The story can be completely fictitious or an accounting of a real event. Be very descriptive about the physical aspects of the scene. It will add a new dimension of perception for your reader. "While standing in the shower this morning, I remembered the time we were caught in that storm in Louisiana. As I held you close, feeling the warm bayou rain falling on my shoulders, I thought I could have stood there with you forever." Paint a detailed picture in the reader's mind of the exact smells, sounds, colors, feelings, textures, forms, and placing of objects. With this type of letter, you could hardly go wrong—unless you made your lover the villain of the story.

There are several sources to draw from for story ideas. However, most people have good imaginations when it comes to thinking about their lovers. Remember, there are no rules or people waiting to judge your writing.

If you really get the bug to write a long novel to your lover, we recommend looking for additional reference material specifically for writing novels. You may want to know more about character development, plot turns, etc. You don't have to get technical about it all, but it may help generate new ideas. Your best reference for ideas will most likely be novels you have already read. Better yet is a novel your reader has read and liked.

Lust and Yearning

You've been seeing Romeo for months now. The two of you are very compatible, and you find yourself thinking about him more and more — especially his sexuality, which is incredible. You can't get enough of each other, but you just keep trying!

> *Dear Romeo you <u>machine</u> you,*
>
> *Last night was incredible. As was yesterday afternoon, yesterday morning, Thursday night, Thursday afternoon (both times), and Thursday morning. I'd go back even further, but I'd run out of paper. You are an incredible man. I can't think of anything but you and that body of yours. I can't concentrate. People around me are starting to wonder what's wrong with me. The only thing wrong with me is that I'm not in your arms right now. I can hardly wait until tonight.*
>
> *Anticipating your arrival,*
Juliet

These are very natural letters to write. If you believe the scientific data on how much time the average person spends thinking about sex, you will realize the volume of correspondence that could be generated on this subject alone.

These letters are best reserved for people you are already in a good romance with. A lusty letter should not be the first letter you send to your lover. It will be better received if it has been delivered after a few letters of a more innocuous nature.

The temptation to be very graphic may be hard to resist, but elegance is the name of the game for good lusty writing. Colorful use of metaphor will work very well when describing physical attributes.

A lusty letter can describe either a real or imagined scenario. Use your imagination; write about a passionate encounter you've envisioned. As with a novella, describe all the sensory aspects you can think of—the sounds, smells, lighting, textures, and tastes.

A wonderful example of a lusty letter would be a description of a recent rendezvous (involving the reader of your letter, of course). Take the time to articulate the feelings you had at the time. Imagine the object of your desire reading (and rereading) your account of the love between you. You cannot go wrong here!

In a society that makes many feel physically inadequate, be very complimentary of the physical aspects of your lover. Beauty is always in the eye of the beholder. Make sure your love knows what you find appealing. It may help to overlook the obvious and focus on the unique sound of her voice or the tiny specks of brown in his eyes. These kinds of details let your reader know just how strong the attraction is.

Desperation

You've been dating Juliet for five years. You've had your ups and downs, but lately it's been more downs than ups. You seem to be on the brink of breaking up, but the closer you get to a breakup, the more you find yourself resisting the idea. Your good intentions are misunderstood, and you can't seem to communicate how you feel. What can you do to save this relationship?

Juliet, my one and only,

We've had our ups and downs, I know, and it seems that lately things have not been going well between us. I think it's important you know how much I truly love you. I am willing to do anything to make our relationship work. You are the most important thing in my life, and I am not willing to let you go. Please give us another chance.

I love you,
Romeo

This, again, is an extremely difficult situation and not one that anyone wants to be in. Despite this, many people we talked to have found themselves in that position. The story was the same. The relationship started to turn sour. Simple disagreements turned into full-blown arguments complete with threats of leaving and all the verbal abuse that could be invoked. Once this started, it was like falling into a fast moving river. They couldn't get out of the flow even if they wanted to. The turbulence increased until finally the only answer was to end the relationship.

But in one case, they were able to turn the tide. A love letter was the key element in turning what could have been a breakup into a happy reconciliation. One couple we talked to had been going through a tremendous parting of the ways. They were married but hadn't spoken to each other in days. In her mind, the ten-year marriage was over. It seemed all that remained was the physical separation of belongings and finding a new place to live.

Then, when she went out to her car during her lunch hour, she found a letter in her seat. It was from her husband. In the letter, he poured out to her how much he loved her and how much she meant to him. He told her that he hated what was happening to them but didn't know what to do to stop it.

It took just that letter to stop it. She went to him immediately, and they have been together for another eight years since then. They look back at that time as a turning point in their lives. Without that letter, without his pouring out of feelings to her, they would not be together today.

Your relationship does not have to be in the deteriorated shape this relationship was in to write this type of letter. A love letter detailing the importance of someone can be written anytime. But if you find your relationship is at a low point, this type of letter may help.

I'm Sorry!

You and Juliet have been dating each other exclusively for several months now. You've fallen into a very comfortable pattern with each other and both seem satisfied with the relationship — maybe too comfortable, however! Your "one year anniversary of the day we met" was yesterday, and you forgot all about it! Juliet is hurt. How do you apologize to her without sounding flippant?

> *Dear Juliet,*
>
> *Last night I remembered, too late, that the anniversary of our meeting had come and gone. I felt so bad, I wanted to call you immediately but realized it was too late. Instead, I kicked myself*

all night long for being such an unthinking, inconsiderate lug. Please forgive me. I promise to make it up to you on our "one year and one week anniversary of the day we met!" I've made reservations at "our place" for next Friday night.

*Love,
Romeo*

We've all been there. Said or done something dumb, something without thinking, something insensitive or inconsiderate. It certainly doesn't mean you don't love the person you may have hurt. Saying you're sorry helps, of course. But a lot of people we talked to said that a wound is a wound, and an "I'm sorry" doesn't really heal the wound all that quickly. You still usually have to do something else just to make yourself feel better—flowers, a gift, a night out.

Next time this happens, try writing a love letter. Writing down how bad you feel for making that other person feel so bad actually eases the pain both of you may be feeling. You're doing something concrete, something lasting for that other person. You're letting that person know how deep and meaningful the love is, and at the same time you're acknowledging the fact that you acted in an inappropriate way. A thoughtfully written "I'm sorry" is a powerful apology!

The variety and styles of writing are endless, as are the emotions that inspire you to write. Your own personal style will evolve from the feelings you have when you sit down to write your loved one.

Chapter Five
Writing Your Letter

> Why is it that you can sometimes feel
> the reality of people more keenly
> through a letter than face to face?
>
> — Anne Morrow Lindbergh

WITH A PROPER mindset, comfortable surroundings, and knowledge of the elements of passionate correspondence, you are ready to write a letter that would do Cyrano de Bergerac proud. It will be written like all great works of literature—with passion and style. It will charm your reader eternally.

All great letters have certain things in common: a personalized salutation, a powerful message, and a sincere closing. By combining these elements with your heartfelt inspiration, you have the formula for the perfect love letter.

Attention to the little things that occur in a romance is important. Recall the small things and expound upon them in your letter. The effect is charming and shows sincerity and sensitivity. Notice the subtle (or not so subtle) changes in your partner: new hairstyle, new interests, etc. You can write a lot about less significant things (a look she gave you at dinner) if they are more important to you than the epic events (first kiss).

Never Out of Style

Your 25th wedding anniversary is coming up in just a few weeks. You have already purchased a special gift for Romeo but have been unable to find a card that says exactly what you want to say. Two weeks before your anniversary you attend a small gathering at your parents' house for your grandmother's birthday. During the course of the evening, you talk to your grandmother alone. After that conversation, you know exactly what to say to Romeo.

> *My Darling Romeo,*
>
> *When my grandmother met my grandfather 70 years ago, he courted her in a manner proper for the time. The day he asked her to be his wife, she agreed, even though up to that point they had never had any physical contact with one another. After she said yes, he took it upon himself to change all that and leaned in as if to kiss her. She withdrew, still shy so soon after the engagement had begun. He attempted again, and again she pulled back her head, not allowing the kiss. On the third attempt, he reached over and took both ends of the scarf that was*

Salutations

There are many salutations available. The most widely used is "Dear …." With a little imagination you can modify that to:

> *My Dear,… Dearest,… My Dearest,… Darling,… My Darling,… My Love,…*

Other salutations may include a pet name that only you use, a nickname, or a loving title:

> *My Darling Blue-Eyed Wonder,*

Use your imagination and make your greeting personal. Try a different salutation each time while conveying a message:

> *Dear RomeoIThinkILoveYouBrown,*

> *Dear RomeoICanHardlyWaitToSeeYouTonightBrown,*

and

> *Dear RomeoLastNightWasIncredibleBrown,*

all convey thoughts of love and make reading the salutation fun.

What if your boyfriend has German in his heritage, but doesn't have a German name. Each time you wrote him you could change his last name to make it sound German.

> *Dear RomeoBrownenstein,*

> *Dear RomeoBrownschlecken,*

and

> *Dear RomeoAdolfinBrown,*

(the latter if you thought he'd been a dictator about something). Your boyfriend will probably get a kick out of his new names (although we aren't sure how the "Adolf" will be received) and will look forward to what you come up with next.

By using your imagination and creative thinking, you can choose a salutation that will set the tone for the message to come.

My Darling Juliet,

certainly sends a different message than

Juliet You Steam Roller You!

With a little thought about the message you are trying to convey, an appropriate salutation will be easy to find. Remember though, the most beautiful sound to a person is the sound of his or her own name.

The Body

After the salutation, make a statement to set the tone for the letter. A simple "I've been thinking about you" will provide a gentle but powerful entry into your letter. Try beginning a lusty letter with "The dream is always the same." Start with an attention grabbing thought that will allow you to begin painting a picture in your reader's mind.

One of the nice things about a letter is not having to worry about voice tone and body language. The words will stand by themselves as the medium of your thoughts. However, letters can adopt a certain tone depending on the words you choose, and the words you choose will typically reflect your current mood. The next three examples convey entirely different moods and tones.

> *My Dearest Juliet,*
>
> *Not a moment passes that I don't think about how fortunate I am to have shared your intimate company. I am breathless with the anticipation of being in your arms again.*

or,

> *Dear Juliet,*
>
> *I have been thinking about how lucky I am to be your lover. I am looking forward to seeing you again.*

or,

> *Juliet Baby,*
>
> *I can't stop thinking about kissing you from head to toe. When can I do it again?*

Think about the mood and tone you want your letter to convey, and choose your words accordingly.

You have your chance to be creative in the body of your letter. Love letters do not need to be an exercise in your creative abilities but can be if you desire. Even if your letter is a simple note containing only the words "I love you," it will be significant because it is coming from you. However, it is fun and rewarding to create something original. Since this is not business correspondence, you are not concerned about protocol and rules and you can use your freedom to make your letter a work of art.

Be as creative as the situation calls for. Experiment with different writing techniques. You may find one that works for you every time, or you may enjoy using a different approach for each letter. Most important, find a way to harness inspiration before you begin writing your letter. An average person would buy a greeting card with a preprinted message. By reading this book, you've proven you are not an average person. You are a person who wants to create an original memento tailored for a special person, and by using your creative energy you can do just that. There are several ways to make your letter more interesting.

Try writing your letter from a different viewpoint. You could write as if you were something other than human—an animal, a piece of music, a flower on her dresser, her underwear. It'll make your loved one laugh, and you'll have a good time writing it.

Write your letter in a foreign language. This can be challenging, especially if you and your recipient don't speak that language. Language books are available that you can use, or you could get someone to translate. (You might, however, find it inhibiting for someone else to read your letter.) You could simply intermix some foreign words into your letter for fun.

Use humor. Letters need not be serious, but sometimes they get pretty serious when writing about how you feel. If you are a joker by nature, give in to your temptation to make some funnies along the way. Humor could be anything from a funny drawing to a joke about yourself.

Experiment with humility. Humility is a wonderful trait to possess and demonstrate when you are communicating affectionately. Many times it helps to poke a little fun at yourself to get your message across. Humility is not to be mistaken for beating yourself up when you are feeling down. Rather, it should be a product of your sincerity and show your honest feelings about yourself.

Use metaphor. Metaphor is the art of presenting an alien idea or concept in a manner that will be familiar to the reader. When metaphor is used effectively, your reader understands it, and you are demonstrating that you understand how your reader thinks. This is a flattering gesture that will charm your reader. Using metaphor will also make your writing more interesting. Be sure to use terms or phrases your reader is familiar with. Don't describe your relationship in football terms if your partner knows nothing about sports.

Include a picture drawn by hand. Decorate the margins of the paper with something like ivy growing up the side of the letter. If you are feeling humorous, draw a cartoon or comic strip. If you are really talented, you may write your letter in a series of drawings. If you are feeling artistic but don't have the time or ability to include art of your own, include something already made. Try a picture of something dear to your reader like a nature scene or a bouquet of flowers.

Enclose a photograph with the letter. It could be anything from a photo of yourself to a picture of something or somewhere that is significant to you both. You could also include a clipping from a newspaper or magazine, a cartoon, a label, a drawing—anything that might have special meaning for the two of you.

Try calligraphy. This will add a little class to your letter. Calligraphy may resemble the writing you see in **ancient texts**, but the term also applies to any *elegant, artistic handwriting*. It is not as hard as it looks. Many art stores have the supplies you need, including inexpensive beginner kits. A special touch would be to start the letter with one large calligraphy letter, rather than writing the entire letter in calligraphy.

Ending

The ending of your letter is important. It should summarize your feelings. Often, the ending is what will be reread again and again. There are several elegant ways to sign off. Some examples:

> *Love, ... Affectionately yours, ... Your sweetie, ... Forever yours, ... Always devotedly, ... All my love now and forever, ... There, ... Lots of love, ... I kiss you, ... Until I see you again, ... Warmest thoughts, ... Now and Forever, ...*

Many letter writers leave "X's" and "O's" under their name. This custom originated years ago when most people could not read or write. They would sign documents with an "X" and then kiss the "X" on the paper to affirm the mark. Eventually the "X" and the kiss became synonymous. Since hugs and kisses go together, it was natural for the "O" to represent the hug. With a little imagination, the letter "O" resembles the circle formed when your arms are wrapped around someone.

Assuming your reader knows who you are, you may opt to sign off with your location and the date of your letter. You may also use your initials or a nickname. As with the salutations, experiment until you find one that fits. You might even try a different one with each letter, which will leave your reader eager to see what you've come up with each time.

Delivering Your Message

The method for delivering your message can be anything from dropping it in a mailbox to having a friend dress up in a gorilla suit and hand deliver it while singing "I'm Ape Over You." If it's short, delivery might be by airplane banner or movie marquee. A long message might be better delivered by courier.

If you would rather not mail your letter, there are creative alternatives. You may elect to hand deliver it with a bouquet of flowers or candy. You may also leave it in your loved one's lunchbox or briefcase. You might choose to sneak it into the car, put it under a pillow, tape it to the bathroom mirror, or stick it in with the coffee beans to be discovered early in the day.

You could leave a trail of love notes for your reader that leads them to someplace special—a restaurant or a romantic spot in a park—or maybe your bedroom! When you are feeling creative, you can make it into a treasure hunt by leaving clues as to the location of the next letter. If you are waiting for your lover, don't make the clues too difficult as you may be waiting for some time.

Use your imagination when delivering the message, just as you did when writing it. Any way you get your letter to your loved one will be appreciated, but here are more ideas for making the delivery as special as the letter itself.

Sealing

Sealing your envelope with a kiss is interesting if you are a lady wearing brightly colored lipstick. If you are a man and choose to seal the envelope with a kiss… well, that might be interesting too. Using a wax seal is a special way to seal the envelope. You can also try some original artwork on the outside of the envelope, a cartoon, rubber stamps, even potato art (homemade stamp using a potato and paint).

When sealing your letter, leave the corners open so your reader can use a letter opener. A fun sticker on the flap will also help secure the contents inside the envelope. A wax seal will help (although using a wax seal will not endear you to the post office sorting machines), but it should not be used exclusively; use the glue on the flap as well.

Scenting the letter is another good way to evoke memories in the mind of your recipient. Be sure to select a scent that you wear often—you don't want Juliet remembering George if your name is Romeo! Also, be careful not to smear the ink when moistening the letter.

Mailing Your Letter

The mail system is the most common way to deliver your message. However, you can do several things to make it more than ordinary.

Using a commemorative stamp shows your recipient how much you care. The "LOVE" stamp is one example of a stamp that would convey your special meaning. But if all you have is your ordinary current issue stamp, don't despair—the inverted (upside-down) stamp has historically meant "I love you."

If you're in a foreign country, sending your letter through their postal system, using their stamps, is a nice touch. People enjoy looking at foreign stamps, and it tells your reader you thought enough about them while you were away to make the effort. Don't forget to mail the letter before you leave the country!

There are several post offices in the United States where your correspondence can be specially stamped. This is usually done around Valentine's Day (especially in Loveland, Colorado), but can be done any time of the year. After writing your letter, seal it inside a stamped envelope and address it to your loved one. Next, put this envelope inside another larger envelope addressed to the Postmaster of the post office where you would like it stamped. For example:

Postmaster
Loveland, CO 80537

The Postmaster opens the outer envelope, removes your stamped letter, stamps the letter with the official stamp of the post office, and mails the letter to its final destination. Your lover will then receive your letter with a special postmark. When you try this, send the letter to the Postmaster a week or two before you'd like the letter delivered to your love. "Romantic" postmarks include the following:

Bliss, New York 14024
Bridal Veil, Oregon 97010
Kissimmee, Florida 32741
Loving, New Mexico 88256
Loveland, Colorado 80537
Valentine, Nebraska 69201
Valentine, Texas 79854

Remember, even if you live with the person you are writing to, mailing the letter instead of hand delivering it makes the letter more than just an ordinary piece of correspondence. You may also mail it to their workplace. Generally speaking, the more unusual, the better. It sends the message that the recipient is someone special.

Chapter Six
Some Real Letters

Words make love with one another.

— Andre Breton

WHAT WOULD a book on love letters be if it didn't contain actual letters from real people? This was a very rewarding part of writing this book. Most people we talked to were a bit shy about sharing their letters, but you could tell by the blushing and giggling they were pleased and flattered to be included. How wonderful to be able to pull out your old love letters and share them with other people. We hope you enjoy the next few stories as much as we did and that they help you in your own creative letter writing.

To Polly

Jim and Polly met when Jim asked his buddy, Norman, if Norman's girlfriend had any sisters. She did; in fact she had 11 sisters, but she decided to set Jim up with Polly because the two sisters were waitresses at the same coffee shop. The two met, dated, and fell in love. Jim wrote the following letters to Polly in the months to come.

12 Oct. 53

Dearest Popalina,

Hello my sweetheart! I hope this reaches you real soon. I love you very much, My Darling. In fact, "you'll never know" how much.

We made it back safely, soundly, and with piece of mind. We got back at 12:30. I don't think we'll be up again until the first. The money just went kerpoof!

I have been washing my clothes tonight. I had two full machines. They are done washing and I have one load in the dryer now. In another 30 minutes, that will be dry, then I just have one more load.

Sweetheart, in the last few letters you have written me, you always call me James. Now

James is a fine, fitting, and proper name. I am quite proud of it. Both my father and grandfather, besides your father's, name is James. As I have already said, I like it very much. Now I have just one little request. Could you possibly call me Jim? If you cannot call me Jim, and you must call me James, it is OK.

Sweetheart, I want to marry you next summer. Please say yes, as I can hardly stand being away from you, and if we were married, I could be with you. Or I should say you would be with me. Service life isn't bad for married people, anyway, not when in the Air Force. Of course, in the Army, Navy and Marines, it isn't as easy, because they don't get the same privileges that we in the Air Force do. If you would only consider it. Think it over.

There, I have my washing all done, dried, and folded.

Well my Darling, I shall close for now.

Your Ever Lovin',
Jim

P.S. — I love you

10 May 54

Hello Darling,

Sorry I haven't been able to write much lately, but I have had a rather bad time — Guard duty! It is all over with now, so maybe I can get something done.

I go back on day shift Wednesday morning. I have C.2. tonight, so I am off tomorrow. Maybe I can get a few days leave, and we can get married. Do you have your blood test yet? I hope you do. It might be able to save us some time.

I am afraid I have another long night ahead of me. Just another 12 hours now. Only trouble, I've run out of reading materials. I've read Colliers and Saturday Evening Post. I think I'll take your letters out and read each one of them again — only for the 100th time.

I've got to go before the Commanding Officer tomorrow. I have to request permission to get married. If things work out right, I'll be up to Waco tomorrow night. Then again, if I can't get a leave, I may be forced to wait until Saturday night. I am quite sure of getting a leave though. Then we can be married Friday or Saturday, or even before!

I'll close now Darling
Jim

18 May 54

Hello My Darling Wife,

How does that sound? I made it back to the base without any trouble. I have been spending most of today putting my clothes away. I didn't get any sleep last night, so I'll get to bed early tonight. I miss you already, Sweetheart. I sure do wish I didn't have to come back to the base when I did. I wanted to stay with you.

Well, Mrs. Hilton, you realize that I love you very much. More than you'll ever dream of, in fact.

Goodnight my Darling Wife,

Your Loving Husband,
Jim

Jim and Polly are celebrating their 40th wedding anniversary next year. When we asked Polly if she had any love letters lying around anywhere, she giggled like a school girl, then retrieved them from her safe deposit box and sent them via certified mail. It's obvious how proud she is of those letters. She told us that after she retrieved them, she reread them and remembered once again those early days of love and longing — proof that the written word will always be cherished and treasured long after the spoken word is forgotten.

To Dorothy

Dorothy is a woman who shows a remarkable ability to fold people into her life, making them feel like they're a part of her own family. The love and concern she displays for others is legendary. The following letters are from people who felt compelled to put in writing how important she is to them.

Grandma,

I ALWAYS like to come and see you. You are VERY fun to be with. I like it when we go into town and when we go to the beach. I know you aren't my real grandma, but I don't remember my other grandma so I think of you as my real grandma, and I always will. I LOVE YOU!

Always,
Megan

Dear Dorothy,

Your retirement party was a great tribute to someone who deserves it. Your kids have inherited your talent for throwing a wonderful party. I have always admired the way you could put together a gathering, make it look beautiful, make your guests feel warm and welcome, and still be calm, cool, and collected.

I think what I admire the most is how you're always there for your family. There is a definite closeness between all of you. I hope I can be the same for mine.

Thanks for always including us and being there when I've needed advice and support. I think my Dad and all of us are fortunate to have you in our lives. I do appreciate you.

Love,
Char

Dorothy,

You said to me, of my newborn, "Of course his eyes will stay blue, we all have blue eyes..." so much have I felt a part of your family and embraced by your love.

You are my "Mom B." You have cooked for me, counseled me and loved me like a daughter. I have laughed and been teased (always) in your home. I have always been welcome since I was smaller than my own child is now.

To write that I love you is too simple and yet it is so very basic.

I love you like a mother because you have always shown me the love and concern that is so much a part of who you are.

Diane

To Julie

Brian is a 35 year old helicopter pilot in the Air Force. He and his wife, Julie, have been together for 19 years. When we asked Julie if she had any love letters she'd like to share, she searched through several boxes of correspondence before admitting she had none. She said of the many letters she received from Brian during his frequent assignments overseas, not one could be classified as a love letter. She seemed despondent about that, and mentioned it to Brian. He apparently did some soul searching, because when Julie's birthday arrived a month later, she found he had written the following in her birthday card:

> Jul,
>
> Every year I fall more and more in love with you. You've been a wonderful wife, mother, and best friend. I do love and appreciate you so very much, though I'm not all that good at telling you like I should. I hope you know that is the way I feel in my heart and always will.
>
> Looking forward to the next 19 years plus the next 19 years and maybe even one more set of 19 years!
>
> Love,
> Bri

As Julie sat at the kitchen table, silently reading her birthday card while her family looked on, her eyes filled with tears over the loving words Brian had finally put down on paper.

To Mike

Mike and Jennifer met at work during a brown-bag lunchtime seminar. In their mid-thirties, they are both career-minded individuals who had never been in love. Their meeting was unplanned, and the resulting love affair took them both by surprise. When Mike left for a month-long business trip after they had been seeing each other for almost a year, Jennifer wrote him the following love letter:

> Dear Mike,
>
> You're not there yet and I'm already writing to you! Oh well, I just thought you'd like to get some mail pretty soon, and I felt like writing. Which is pretty amazing, since I've been writing for hours (work)!
>
> I hope you had a nice trip. Are you adjusting nicely? Or did you love it immediately? How's work? What's your schedule look like? I know what you're thinking, you're thinking "Any more questions Jennifer?" Actually, I could probably think of lots more, but I'll ask just one — do you miss me yet? I miss you! ("I miss you more..." "No, I miss YOU more...")
>
> I love you. Love and Kisses, sweetie,
>
> Jennifer

When Mike returned from his business trip (with a briefcase full of love letters from Jennifer), he proposed to Jennifer at the airport. They have been happily married for five years.

To Linda

Don and Linda were friends for several years before they started dating. The transition into a romantic relationship was sometimes rocky. This letter reflects a period of time in the relationship when it was unclear as to whether they would be friends or lovers.

> Hi Sweetie,
>
> Just got back from "Silence of the Lambs." Sure hope I can sleep tonight. Hate to miss out on dreamin' of you. Got your postcard from Rhode Island. Sorry to hear the weather is not so good. If it's any help, it's not very good here either.
>
> Work is still going well, although I probably won't be coming back out here for awhile. That's okay. I'm not fond of the thought of leaving you again. I feel bad that we didn't see more of each other at the beginning of the year. Even though we are not officially "going together," we have still managed to see a lot of each other. I like that.
>
> I like it more when we are going out. I find you so attractive and irresistable. I can't stand just being friends. It seems unnatural. However, we will always be friends no matter what happens on the romantic front.
>
> The message is the same. I love you and miss you. I'm counting the days.
>
> > I love you Linda!
> > Don

Don and Linda continued their uncertain relationship for several months, then decided to be "just friends." Today, five years after the attempt at an intimate relationship, Don and Linda are still friends. They attribute their continued friendship to the open communication they experienced through letter writing.

To Sandy

Scott and Sandy met at a mutual friend's birthday party. From the beginning, they were physically attracted to one other. After several months of an intense physical relationship, Scott wrote the following to Sandy:

> My Most Desirable Sandy,
>
> It's a cool foggy evening here on the coast. I'm sipping some Amaretto and listening to the mellow sounds of Wes Montgomery's guitar. You probably think I'm in the typical "Scott relax mode." That is true. I need it. For the past few weeks, I cannot seem to think straight. The better part of my working day is spent on one thought: seducing you.
>
> I know we once said "no regrets," but I wish I would never have known your passion. The affect is narcotic to say the least. The temptation of your charm is too much to ask a mortal man like me to resist.
>
> Even simple things like taking you to dinner are becoming fantasies too wild to describe. My recent invite was genuine and innocent. However, desire has gotten the best of me.

I plan to rent a limo on your birthday and take you out for a quiet romantic dinner. I can picture you sitting across from me, sipping white wine, enjoying the cuisine, and looking irresistable in a button-up-the-front dress. The conversation will be, as always, delightful.

As the meal ends, the waiter will ask if we want any dessert. I will ask for a slice of cheesecake—to go. There will be a curious look on your face as you ask me "Why not eat it here?" My reply—"I'll have it later."

I will instruct the driver to take us down the coastal highway, towards home. As the long white car cruises down the coast with the stereo playing John Klemmer, I will remove the cheesecake from the foil. I will then unbutton your dress, thereby revealing the lines of your beautiful form: the subject of my most ardent physical desire. I will remove your undergarments and place the dessert on your firm stomach. I know I won't be able to finish even one bite. You can imagine what happens next. No matter what, you will melt with that cheesecake before we make it home.

I could write you a hundred more letters like this, but I don't know if I should even mail this one.

Scott

Scott did deliver the letter to Sandy, and his fantasy came true. When her birthday arrived, so did the limo and cheesecake!

To Brent

Angela moved into Brent's neighborhood while they were in high school, but because Brent's dad was in the military, Brent moved away a month after they met. The two started writing to each other, and continued writing for the next four years. When Brent finished high school, he enlisted in the Navy.

> Brent,
>
> I just received your letter this morning. I'm really glad to get another one so soon.
>
> It's good hearing you are doing well at boot camp. I was told it wasn't easy. Just try and do your best always. Know that I'm thinking about you often.
>
> This time your letter really touched me. It means so much that you are looking forward to seeing me. I can't wait until May. I wish I could see you graduate, then go to Disney World with you. I know it's impossible, but I can still dream of it.
>
> Oh Brent, if only you hadn't moved as soon as you did. I wish we could have gotten to know each other better. I started liking you so much before you left. I can remember going swimming and you chasing me all around the pool.
>
> I'm thinking about you and miss you.
>
> > Love Always,
> > Angela

When Brent finished boot camp, he and Angela were finally reunited after over four years apart! Angela wrote the following letter to Brent when the weekend was over:

> *Hey My Luv,*
>
> *How's life there? Lonesome here! I miss you so much Brent! I think about the weekend over and over again. It was the best weekend I have ever had. I wish there was a way to turn the days back a little and start from late Friday night.*
>
> *I can't wait to hear from you again. I'm trying not to be depressed, but I can't help what love has done to me. I miss my sailor so much, and that's all there is to it. It's love!*
>
> *It was so hard saying goodbye to you Monday night. I thought it would be. I know it's going to be awhile before I can be with you again. I often wonder what it would have been like if you hadn't moved, and I wish you lived closer now.*
>
> *Write me soon. I miss you!*
>
> *Love You,*
Angela

Angela and Brent were still in their teens when the Navy sent Brent to the opposite coast. He wanted Angela to come with him, but because of their age, they finally decided against it. They have remained friends, and every once in awhile think back to their long-distance love affair and the letters that carried them through it all.

To Tiffany

Trey is a 24 year old college student. He is an amicable young man who went from one job to another after high school until he got a job at a local restaurant. He had never had a serious relationship or done anything that could even remotely be considered romantic. Then he met Tiffany, a part-time student studying psychology at the local university. Tiffany turned Trey's life upside down. After only six months of dating, Trey presented the following poem to her:

Nothing to Offer But Love

To the girl I'm in love with unconditionally,
The same girl I'm in sync with traditionally,
I've not much to offer for your birthday,
for I'm just a poor Texas farm boy named Trey.

Though I cannot this day offer you a ring,
I promise you that the future it will bring.

Instead I offer you these roses,
In case you're feeling blue,
I hear they have a special meaning,
And I believe it's "I love you."

Although I cannot offer you a ring,
Or even a ride in a horse-driven carriage,
I pray that in your eyes I'm not too bold,
As I ask your hand in marriage.

Love,
Trey

Trey and Tiffany were married 3 months later. As a wedding gift to Tiffany, Trey had his poem copied and enlarged in calligraphy, the dozen roses dried, and both framed in a beautiful shadow box which was displayed proudly at their wedding reception by a glowing Tiffany. When Tiffany relayed the story of their meeting and subsequent courtship, nothing was recanted with more pride and love than when she said, "Trey wrote this poem for me!"

To Karl

Karl's brother-in-law's sister's best-friend, Jill, came to a family gathering on the 4th of July, since her family was in Wisconsin. When she and Karl met, they hit it off right away and decided they wanted to spend every 4th of July together (as well as every other day). Unfortunately, the very next 4th of July, Jill had to fly to Wisconsin for her youngest sister's baby shower. She wrote the following love note to Karl:

> *i miss your face so much, and your hugs and kisses too — xxxo — i think about you lots and if i close my eyes, i can think about your face when you're sleeping, and when i come home and when you're wiggling around — xxxo — it's so nice to wake up to you in the morning — i like to lay there and cuddle. i can't wait to come home. miss you lotsa! lov - me*

Karl loved the note, but they agreed that the next baby shower in Wisconsin would be enjoyed by both of them!

To Colleen

Colleen and Dan were both artists who met and fell in love in high school. After graduating, Colleen decided to go to Belgium for a year to continue her studies. She and Dan had a relationship based soundly on friendship and the fact that they were both artists. He was a quiet, inner person, but when Colleen was leaving, he presented her with a letter to tell her just what he was feeling.

> Colleen,
>
> This is my good-bye note. I hope the best for you. I know what a little bit of traveling did for me, and I expect being away will be good for you as well. I'm not worried that you will make the best of it. You will probably see things shrink down to size. The world looks big from a small valley. I have a feeling you will learn a lot in many ways, and I respect your strength and determination in going.
>
> I want you to know how much I will miss your friendship. I am not going to be waiting for you to come back. I expect a lot of change in both of us. However, it would be a lie to say you won't be on my mind. I know I will miss you. You have qualities I look for in people and rarely find. I will miss the fine person that only you are. I love you.
>
> I hope you find a creative environment for your work.
>
> > Love,
> > Dan

After several months of being apart, he wrote again, this time revealing even more about his feelings:

> Colleen
>
> No one has told me less and given me more then you have. You are hard to write to because words weren't what we based our friendship on, so I hope you can feel these words as they are intended to be felt.
>
> I am glad I looked at you as hard as I did before you left. Your eyes were warm inside. I can value that warmth for a long time. I don't mean so much as your feelings towards me, as your own personal warmth which I can remember. I am not one to harp on memories. Memories hold time and time cannot be held, but I do want to hold onto some of these.
>
> I have a feeling of freedom and a feeling of loneliness. Freedom because there is nothing here in this valley to hold me. Loneliness because you are not here to fill the slow hours.
>
> Love,
> Dan

Dan and Colleen continued their long-distance relationship while Colleen was in Belgium and for several years after she returned. The relationship eventually ended as they grew older and their interests changed. Today, 16 years after her trip to Belgium, Colleen is a graphic artist with her own business, and Dan is a successful and well-known artist. They are both married with children, and are still friends. Colleen treasures her letters from Dan and the memories they evoke.

To Lynn

Brian is in his early thirties and has experienced love a number of times in his life. The experiences, while memorable, were not always lasting. Then, while giving a presentation on making margaritas during a business seminar, he met Lynn. Lynn was interested in his recipe and a romance quickly ensued. When Lynn went away on a business trip, he wrote the following letter:

> *My Dearest Lynn,*
>
> *It was so nice to hear your voice on Saturday. I knew your journey was safe, but I couldn't help worrying a little. I suppose it's because I always visualize you at home or at work distracting your male co-workers. Ha-Ha. I guess I'll just think of you gracing Europe with your beauty and charm for the next couple of weeks.*
>
> *I think of you often with great warmth and desire. Your appeal is limitless. I think you are a very beautiful woman, but that is only a small part of my attraction to you. I have great respect for your maturity and intelligence. I enjoy the talks we have had together. I love the way you look at me and the sound of your sweet sexy voice. I cannot get enough of it. You have such a soothing effect on me, I can't imagine being without you. It seems I am no longer able to resist your affection.*

Awhile back I told you I enjoyed being by myself and that I never got lonely. That has changed. I know I would be very lonely if you were not in my life. Therefore, it seems I am spending most of my time thinking of ways to make sure that doesn't happen.

You are the most wonderful person I have ever known. You flatter me constantly with all the nice things you say. I admire the balance you have in your life: beauty, passion, intelligence, culture, the list goes on. From you I am learning much about how wonderful it is to love and be loved.

I hope your feelings toward me continue to grow. No matter what happens between us over the years, I will always love and support you. I know this to be true because our romance is much more than the day to day attraction we have for each other. That is what will make our relationship endure.

Love you always,
Brian

Today, Brian is a co-author of "When Romeo Wrote Juliet," and is engaged to Lynn. Their wedding is planned for next spring.

To Jeff

Paula is a woman in her late thirties who has experienced love a number of times in her life. The experiences, while memorable, were not always lasting. Then, while attending a meeting at work, she met Jeff. Jeff was different from any man she had ever been involved with, and after a brief period of friendship, a romance ensued. While Jeff was fixing the VCR in the other room, she wrote the following letter:

> *Dear Jeff,*
>
> *A lot of people have been asking me about the Romeo and Juliet stories. They want to know who they are, where they live and why do I know so much about them. I answer that you are my Romeo, I am your Juliet, and we live in our own castle in California. That I know so much about them because little bits and pieces of our lives have snuck into those tales.*
>
> *Your love breathed life into my make-believe Romeo and Juliet. Without your love, I could not possibly have found the inspiration to imagine these people and the profound effect they have on one another. Because in my life, you have had that very effect on me.*
>
> *Love and thanks,*
Paula

Today, Paula is a co-author of *When Romeo Wrote Juliet*. She and Jeff live together with their children in their castle in California and couldn't be happier!

Chapter Seven
Summary and Closing Thoughts

> Why do writers write?
> Because it isn't there.
>
> — Thomas Berger

*L*OVE IS an extraordinary emotion. You experience the highest highs, the lowest lows, and every emotion in between. When love is at its peak, colors seem intensified, the air seems clearer, stars shine brighter, and all is right with the world.

Sharing your love is a natural extension of being in love, and sharing via the written word is incredibly rewarding. The time and effort you put into your letters of love will be appreciated, even by the most hardened of hearts. The sincere affection and positive feelings you record will be read many times.

We often talked to people with stories about a love letter that was the turning point in their relationship. Perhaps the relationship was on the way out—maybe it had become stagnant, boring, predictable. Adding the element of a love letter changed all that.

The essence of our book is the belief that love is truly inspirational. Briefly focusing this inspiration into writing will produce a letter of permanence and distinction to delight your reader. Your affectionate thoughts will be in evidence for a lifetime.

We hope that our book has given you ideas to make your love experience an even better one. We wish you well in your writing and hope we helped in some small way.

We plan to revise and update this book as we find more fun ideas and true love stories to share. We'd love to include yours. If you would like to share a story or an idea about writing affectionately, please feel free to write us at the following address:

>**Stylus Publishing**
>**When Romeo Wrote Juliet**
>P.O. Box 2741
>Sunnyvale, CA 94087-0741

Appendix
Tools and Materials

FUNDAMENTALLY, a simple pen and paper will suffice for writing. However, your provisions for creating a love letter may reflect different moods, styles, and attitudes. There are a myriad of supplies available to the writer. Taking the time to pick out something fun and worthwhile for your correspondence definitely adds to the charm of writing such a special letter.

With a little shopping around in stationery stores and novelty shops, you can find a large variety of papers, pens, and other accessories. Many excellent writing supplies can be obtained by mail order as well. Some stores even specialize in certain items such as fine pens or rubber stamps.

Using personal letterhead stationery and a beautiful fountain pen may enhance the mood of writing, but if a crayon and the back of an old envelope are the only things handy when you feel that immediate need to express yourself, grab that crayon and put it to work.

Pens, Etc.

There are several types of pens, pencils, and other markers to write with. A quill pen will add to the romance of writing, while paint pens are pure fun. If you collect fine objects, writing love letters can be your excuse to buy yourself a quality fountain pen.

When shopping for a writing instrument, the most important criterion is functionality. It should rest comfortably in your hand and be well balanced. It should leave a nice dark line as you write, without your having to mash the pen against the paper (as you do when writing carbon copies)—bold lines for bold statements. You want your reader to be able to read your affectionate words with no eyestrain. We recommend using fountain pens or rollerball pens (also known as "rolling ball" pens). They both write very nicely, leaving dark legible lines with little effort.

Be sure to try out a fine pen before you buy it. The criteria for your style is very personal. A fountain pen as big as a Cuban cigar may make writing fun and enhance one person's creative thinking, but it could be cumbersome for someone else. "Test drive" a few, and buy a pen that allows your creative process to take control. It's difficult to be creative when your hand is aching! Also be aware that most pens come in a variety of point sizes. The most common sizes are very fine, fine, and medium. Again, keep your personal style in mind when choosing your point size.

When you are in the market for a fine pen, be prepared to pay more than you would for the standard throwaway you borrowed from the office. Nice ballpoints and rollerballs will start around $25 while good fountain pens with well made gold nibs will start at $60. Several of the best pens are $100 to $300 or more. A good pen will last you a lifetime if you take care of it. Once you own a quality pen and get accustomed to using it, you will have a difficult time going back to the inexpensive pens you may have been using before.

Fountain pens. Fountain pens are truly the elegant tools for the romantic writer. Nothing feels quite like a fine fountain pen gliding across a piece of linen paper. Fountain pens tend to individualize each person's writing style. It can be compared to a good perfume that smells one way in the bottle, then seems to change on each person who wears it.

In recent history, fountain pens were the only type of pen you could obtain that would hold ink internally. That was considered quite an advance over dipping the pen tip into the inkwell every few sentences. Since the invention of the ballpoint pen, fountain pens have become more of a distinguished novelty than a practical day-to-day writing device. However, many people still enjoy the pleasure of collecting and writing with fountain pens, and there are clubs and magazines devoted to the hobby.

When looking for a fountain pen, pay particular attention to the material the nib is made of. A high quality fountain pen will typically cost $60 or more because the nibs are made of gold. A gold nib is softer and will write more smoothly than the steel nibs found on less expensive pens. There are also fountain pens designed especially for left-handed people.

One important thing to remember about fountain pens is that they must be broken in for a particular writer. This typically takes about 8 hours of writing. Once they have been broken in properly, they have a feel like a comfortable old shoe. You should not lend it out to anybody else or the nib may be ruined permanently.

Fountain pens are available in many stationery shops and add an elegance to letter writing that can't be described. Look for one that enhances your creative thinking when writing passionately.

Alternative Pens

Older style pens. Instruments such as cane pens, Roman metal pens, Egyptian reed pens, steel pens, quill pens, and the stylus represent writing instruments of the past. The practice of dipping the end of the instrument in an inkwell and writing a few sentences is very old fashioned and lends to the romantic aspect of writing. You may find these instruments in specialty stationery stores and art supply stores.

Calligraphy pens. Even if you are not skilled in the art of calligraphy, you could create a very nice letter with minimum practice. Calligraphy pens are similar to fountain pens in that they have a nib and use ink. Each nib has a different shape to give a different line as you write. These pens are typically found in art stores. Inexpensive kits are available that contain several different sizes and types of nibs.

Paint pens. Paint pens normally come with gold or silver ink and leave a heavy reflective line, which makes them excellent for writing on dark stationery. Gold ink on black paper will definitely get your reader's attention. The ink is very wet (compared to that of a ballpoint) and will soak through thin paper, so be sure to use thick paper when using a paint pen.

Glass pens. If you have a flair for the extravagant, there are pens made entirely of glass. The ends are composed of several strands of very fine glass that have been tapered together to form a tip similar to a No. 9 oil paint brush. To use the pen, you dip it into an inkwell and start writing, as with a quill. They are sturdy and elegant. Glass pens require more care than traditional pens. They don't take kindly to tapping on desks or going through the washer. This is something you may have to adjust to if you're used to using a 19¢ throwaway.

Pencils. Pencils are very functional as writing instruments but more useful for adding an artistic touch to your letters if you like to draw. Because of the fuzzy line they leave, pencils are normally harder to read and therefore not as good as pens. Additionally, writing with a pencil leaves you with the temptation to edit, erase, and rewrite your letter. Since you are writing a love letter, not a draft term paper, this is usually not good practice. Pencils come in a variety of types and grades, so if you do decide to use one, make sure it writes dark and legibly.

Typewriters

Since the advent of computers and word processors, many people say they use typewriters primarily to fill out preprinted forms and perform similar tasks. That's not to say that's the only thing they're good for, however! If you think best with a typewriter at your fingertips, then find a typewriter and let those fingers fly! Many people type faster than they can write, but since you will not be in a race to compose a love letter (unless this is one of those love triangle things), speed should not be a factor when determining what to write with.

Our own personal feeling is that typewriters can be used for composing the letter, but a handwritten letter is preferable. Personal feelings aside, you can find good, inexpensive typewriters in office supply and second-hand stores.

Computers

Even though we have stated spontaneity and handwriting are important, you can use a computer to compose your letters. Computers add a new dimension to the art of correspondence. For the purpose of generating love letters, they can be either useful or problematic. A computer is like any other writing instrument (only much more expensive) and should be used if it enhances your ability to write passionately. However, too much capability may produce a document that is sterile and uninviting. Many people feel that a handwritten love letter is more personal.

Computers are the tools of the information age and are great for business. They are efficient and practical for generating official documentation and information. Technically, love letters are information, but the data is of a very special and personal nature.

The advantages of using a computer are many. In addition to being environmentally safe, computers allow you to manipulate several of the mechanical aspects of writing quickly and easily. You can type the letter, edit it as you write, check the spelling with a spell checker, check your grammar with a grammar checker, and format the words on the page in the exact spots you'd like those words to appear.

In addition, you can **vary** the *fonts*, add ☞graphics♥, use **bold**, *italic*, and underlining to emphasize key words or phrases, even cut and paste from one love letter to the next (if you happen to be writing more than one love letter at a time).

One of the best uses of computers as they relate to correspondence is electronic mail (E-mail). E-mail is a process whereby you type your message into a computer and send it to another computer. The advantage of this type of mail is that it happens very quickly. When someone sends you a message, it normally gets to you within minutes. The message will wait until the receiver reads it at the computer terminal. It can normally be printed out as well. Once the message has been read, it is very easy to reply and continue a warm written dialogue with your loved one.

Another advantage of E-mail is the ability to instantly send and receive messages with someone traveling. If your love is traveling with a computer used to log into a mail system, you can leave messages to be read later. This is especially nice if the trip is too short or has too many different stops to make using the normal mail practical.

There are several networks that provide E-mail. Some are sponsored by user groups or universities and are virtually free. Other commercial on-line services charge by the hour and are relatively inexpensive. You simply log on to upload and download your mail, which only takes seconds of chargeable time. Remember, though, that privacy on E-mail systems is never guaranteed.

The advantages to using a computer are numerous, but it should also be noted that some problems could arise from this capability. For instance, you may find you've ended up with a love letter that looks like a business memo, complete with all the jargon of your trade. Or, it may be unreadable due to too many different fonts, too many emphasized words and phrases, and excessive graphics. Worse yet, your affectionate correspondence may resemble a form letter, complete with even edges, page numbering, and generic sentences that convey nothing but good form.

The look of a handwritten love letter can be very appealing. Like a fine piece of art, it distinguishes itself by having all the markings of an original work. Even if the handwriting is slightly hard to read, the letter shows a personal character and style that is lacking in computer output.

A good compromise would be to compose your letter on a computer, then print it out. With the printout in hand, you can spend your writing time crafting a beautiful document. With good penmanship, exotic pens and papers, and possibly a few drawings, your letter will be complete.

Papers, Etc.

Now that we've taken an in-depth look at what's available to write with, let's examine our options when determining what to write on. You are certainly not limited to plain white paper. You can find paper in every color of the rainbow, or you can use blank greeting cards or personalized stationery.

There are many excellent papers available for your writing pleasure. They come in different colors, textures, finishes, and weights and range from the very reasonable to the very expensive. Some can be purchased by the individual sheet, others sell by the pound. Many of the paper characteristics are more the serious concern of the graphic artist, not the average letter writer. Even though we don't have to concern ourselves with all the details, here are a few facts to note.

Color is a wonderful way to personalize your letter and convey that special thought or feeling that just can't be put across any other way. In researching this book, we've found everything from jet black to fluorescent orange to a myriad of earth tones. Think about your intentions, then choose your color accordingly.

The weight of a particular paper is another characteristic to consider. Some papers are so thin you can see through them, like Oriental rice paper. Other paper is as thick as a postcard, such as card stock. When selecting your paper, consider how the weight of the paper affects you and decide whether or not it will have the same impact on your reader.

The finish of a paper describes how it reflects light and is closely tied to the texture of paper. Some papers are coated to provide a highly reflective "glossy" look. This paper will feel quite smooth, and is commonly used to produce brochures with pictures. Most writing papers are not glossy.

Many writers stick with the same stationery year after year. One person we spoke with always writes on purple stationery. It is her "signature," giving her letters a special personal touch that allows them to be recognized immediately as hers. You may find that pulling out your own special stationery takes you out of your normal mode and puts you immediately into a creative mindset.

Papermaking. As a side note, some people like to make their own paper. This may seem extreme, but it can also be a lot of fun. Local colleges, community centers, and art stores typically host classes in the craft of paper making. The paper produced in these classes is not like the paper you normally buy. You will not be making 500 sheets of white bond at once. Instead, the paper is crafted a sheet at a time using different materials to achieve a variety of colors, textures, and finishes. Since each batch is handmade, the paper is unique and has the singular qualities of the person who made it—just another touch in crafting a one-of-a-kind letter.

Personalized Stationery

Once reserved only for the affluent, many people today can afford a nice stationery set made from fine paper with their name and address embossed at the top. Although you might not think of going this far for your personal writing materials, it adds a nice touch to your letter. If you have a computer and a good printer, you can make your own stationery and even include a personal message.

For example:

> From the loving hand of Romeo to Juliet

printed across the top of the page would certainly get your attention (especially if your name were Juliet).

A local stationery store can help you select a letterhead that fits your style and budget. Normally they will have a catalog of stock designs and fonts to choose from. If you desire to create your own stationery design using a special emblem or multiple colors, you may have to visit a printer. There is normally an extra cost when creating custom stationery. But, considering the significance of your correspondence, the cost may be of little importance.

Blank Cards

Blank greeting cards are excellent for jotting a quick love note. They can be found in greeting card shops, bookstores, coffee shops, art museums, and a number of other places. Most are similar to a typical greeting card except they are blank on the inside, allowing you to write your own message. Others are postcard style, which are less expensive but lack privacy.

Cards can be found with everything from modern graphic designs to pictures of famous art pieces to fine black and white photographs. If you like to travel, you can find cards that are unique to your location. As you find interesting cards, pick them up even if they will not get sent immediately. Send them later when you feel like writing.

The good thing about blank cards is that they are ageless and not necessarily tied to any particular person or subject. Nor do they have to be reserved for love letters. You can also use blank cards for friends' birthdays and other special occasions and write whatever message you'd like. It is much more personal than a ready-made card.

Other Writing Necessities and Extras

Along with fine pens and unusual writing paper, there are several other items that might come in handy when writing love letters. Reference books can help you find just the right word and spell it correctly. Other stationery supplies can be used to decorate your letter and are just for fun!

Dictionary. The dictionary is an indispensable and universal tool for writing. It will help you with spelling, pronunciation, grammar, and definition of the words used to write your letter. Merriam-Webster's Collegiate Dictionary, Tenth Edition, includes the latest slang and expressions. Don't limit yourself to what you know - reach out into brave new words!

Thesaurus. A thesaurus is a book of synonyms, a word-finding tool for finding words with the same or similar meaning. It is valuable for finding the most appropriate words and adding variety to your writing. This, more than anything, will help make your writing more vivid and enjoyable to read.

Researchers have determined the average person uses a vocabulary of around 400 (out of over 400,000) words for 80 percent of verbal communication. This is not much working material when you consider the multitude of things people have to say to one another. Given that fact, remember that there are always several ways to phrase things, so be creative. Pick words that are unique to the feeling you are trying to communicate. Strive to make your prose as elegant as the occasion warrants.

The "Glossary of Affectionate, Amorous, Descriptive, Exciting, Passionate, and Emotional Words" in the back of this book is a "shopping list" of words that might be appropriate for your love letters. You may have fun just picking several words from this list and writing around them. They may also help you think of other words and phrases to use in your letter. Use your imagination and feel free to add to the list.

Wax Seals

Back in the olden days before glue was invented, paper was folded and sealed using wax. Typically the author of the note had a special seal, unique to himself or his family. It might have been an emblem associated with the family name or another symbol that was recognized as the author's. It was usually kept on his or her person, as a form of identification.

If you want to add a wax seal to your letter, look in stationery and gift stores for the candles and stamps needed. You will find a variety of stamps available, including the letters of the alphabet and recognizable objects such as the sun or animals. A heart, a rose, or lips puckered in a kiss are all appropriate choices.

Adding the wax seal to your letter is a simple process. Seal the envelope in the usual way by licking the flap and pressing it shut. We recommend doing this to ensure the integrity of the contents. Next, place the envelope down on your work space with the flap side up, light a long candle, then tilt it so the flame touches the candle. The wax will then drip off the candle onto your envelope. Let it form a small pool the size of a quarter on the back center of your envelope, then take your stamp and press it into the wax quickly, before it cools. The resulting seal adds beauty and class to your unique letter.

Rubber Stamps

Rubber stamps have become a booming industry in the past few years. Entire stores exist that sell nothing but stamps, ink pads, embossing powders, and associated materials. Most stationery stores, novelty stores, art and craft centers, and even party supply stores carry a large selection of rubber stamps. You can use rubber stamps to decorate your letter or envelope or create your own card. If you have a particular symbol you are associated with ("Kitty" loves cats, or "Dawn" and a rising sun), you'll have no problem finding a stamp with this symbol. You can even have a rubber stamp custom made for you in many of these stores. Decorating your correspondence with a rubber stamp is fun and is an art form in itself. Many of the stamp stores we visited offer lessons in "stamping," but we found they were also happy to answer our many questions on the spot, in lieu of going to class.

Stickers and Graffiti

For an added touch of personality to your correspondence, try adding stickers or graffiti. A man told us that during an extended separation from his girlfriend (now his wife), she faithfully wrote to him, always enclosing a handful of tiny, shiny sequins shaped as hearts, stars, or crescent moons. When he opened the letter, the stuff would come flying out and surprise him every time. He admitted that those letters, sequins intact, are tucked neatly down inside his top drawer, ten years after she sent them to him. Most novelty and stationery stores stock such items to put inside your envelope.

The outside of the envelope can also be decorated. A woman whose husband was stationed overseas always made sure the outside of her letters to him were covered with as much interesting stuff as there was on the inside. Artwork, comics, even P.S.'s add enjoyment and anticipation for your recipient (not to mention the mailman).

Stationery Boxes

Stationery boxes are useful items to keep your materials in. Just like the artist's box, you have a place to store the tools of your craft. Any box will suffice. The economical style would be an old shoe box or a plastic storage box found at any variety store. The other extreme would be a handmade box constructed of exotic wood. If you have a big rolltop desk (the ultimate tool of the serious writer) with lots of drawers, you probably don't need a box. If you don't have a desk, a stationery box is not only practical, but adds credence in your new role as "letter writer extraordinaire!"

Mail Order

If you do not have a large variety of stores where you can shop for your materials, don't worry. Most items can be obtained through mail order companies. By browsing through catalogs, it's possible to find a large variety of pens, for example, that you might not ever find in your local five and dime.

Mail ordering paper and other writing supplies is very convenient for people who have limited time for shopping. It can also be economical, depending on the types and quantities of items you order.

Keep an eye out for unusual paper and interesting accessories as you visit different stores. Pick useful and comfortable materials, and let your heart do the rest.

Mail Order Companies

All companies listed below will send you a catalog (most are free) and will mail writing supplies directly to you.

Stationery Supplies

American Stationery Company
300 Park Avenue
Peru, IN 46970
800-822-2577

Artistic Greetings
409 William Street
Elmira, NY 14902
607-733-6313

Dempsey & Carroll
110 East 57th Street
New York, NY 10022
212-486-7510

Franz Stationery Company, Inc.
1601 Algonquin Road
Arlington Heights, IL 60005
800-323-8685

Merrimade, Inc.
27 South Canal Street
Lawrence, MA 01843
508-686-5511

The Whitewell Company
5850 W. 80th Street
Indianapolis, IN 46268-0186
800-968-5850

Greeting Cards

Current
The Current Building
Colorado Springs, CO 80901
800-525-7170

Kristin Elliott, Inc.
6 Opportunity Way
Newburyport, MA 01950
800-922-1899

Metropolitan Museum of Art
Special Services Office
Middle Village, NY 11381
800-468-7386

Reindeer House
3409 West 44th Street
Minneapolis, MN 55410
800-328-3894

Postage

Philatelic Fulfillment Service Center
U.S. Postal Service
Box 449997
Kansas City, MO 64144-9997

Rubber Stamps, Etc.

Embossing Arts
P.O. Box 626
Sweet Home, OR 97386
503-367-3279

Loving Little Rubber Stamps
2 Spring Street
Stoneham, MA 02180
617-438-8396

Outstamping
P.O. Box 2571
Anaheim, CA 92814
714-535-1593

Stampendous, Inc.
1357 South Lewis Street
Anaheim, CA 92805
714-773-9550 (in Calif.)
800-869-0474 (outside Calif.)

Pens

Bertram's Inkwell
11301 Rockville Pike
Kensington, MD 20895
410-468-6939
800-782-7680

Fountain Pen Hospital
10 Warren Street
New York, NY 10007
800-253-7367
212-964-0580

Hunt Manufacturing Company
230 South Broad Street
Philadelphia, PA 19102
215-732-7700

Menash
462 Seventh Avenue
New York, NY 10018
800-344-7367
212-695-8888

References

Fountain Pens, Vintage And Modern, by Andreas Lambrou. London: Sotheby's Publications. 1989.

Crane's Blue Book of Stationery, Edited by Steven L. Feinberg. New York: Doubleday, 1989

Papermaking, by Jules Heller. New York: Watson-Guptill Publications. 1978

Write Now, by Barbara Getty and Inga Dunbay. Portland, OR: Continuing Education Publications, Portland State University. 1991 (book on improving your handwriting)

The Italic Handwriting Series, by Barbara Getty and Inga Dunbay. Portland, OR: Continuing Education Publications, Portland State University. 1986

The Catalog of Catalogs III, by Edward L. Palder, Rockville, MD: Woodbine House. 1993

Glossary of Affectionate, Amorous, Descriptive, Exciting, Passionate, and Emotional Words!

To help you in creating original love letters, we include some descriptive words to encourage you to express yourself in the language of love. Read through the list, and be sure to add your own when you come up with them!

Adore	I adore the way your nose wrinkles when you laugh.
Affection	My affection for you can no longer go undeclared.
Affinity	I have an affinity for your hazel-blue eyes.
Allure	The allure of your sultry glance is overwhelming.
Appeal	Your appeal is irresistible to a mere mortal like me.
Appreciate	I appreciate your loving and thoughtful ways.
Ardent	I eagerly await your ardent embrace.
Arouse	You arouse my sleeping passion.
Attraction	The attraction between us can no longer be ignored.
Beauty	Your beauty is rivaled by nothing I know.
Bliss	Last night was pure bliss.
Bond	The bond between us is more than physical.
Caring	Your caring ways nourish me.
Caress	I love to caress your supple body.
Charm	Your charm is disarming.
Cherish	I cherish your loving letters.
Closeness	I feel a closeness with you that I've never felt before.
Comfort	I feel comfort from your soothing manner.
Cozy	When I'm with you I feel as cozy as a bug in a rug!
Curvature	The curvature of your body drives me wild.
Delicate	Your delicate kiss incites me.

Delight	I delight in being driven wild by you!
Depth	The depth of my feelings cannot be measured.
Desire	My desire for you is so strong, it changes me.
Devotion	My devotion is true.
Ecstasy	I feel ecstasy in your embrace.
Electrify	You electrify me with your gentle caress.
Elegant	Your elegant way weighs on my mind.
Enchants	Your old-fashioned romantic style enchants me.
Endearing	Your love letters are endearing.
Endure	Our love will endure.
Enliven	Enliven my life, you wench!
Enrapture	Your presence enraptures me.
Enrich	My life is enriched by your companionship.
Essence	You are the essence of my happiness.
Essential	You are essential to my existence.
Esteem	I hold you in the highest esteem.
Fervent	Your fervent kiss drives me wild.
Fondle	I love it when you fondle my toes.
Gentle	Your gentle kiss drives me wild.
Glowing	Do you see me glowing when you're near?
Hearten	I hearten when you say my name.
Heavenly	Your heavenly embrace gives me indescribable happiness.
Important	You are more important to me than pizza.
Infatuated	I was only infatuated with your sister; I love you.
Inspire	You inspire me to greatness.
Intimate	Our intimate moments fill my daydreams.
Joy	You bring joy into my life.
Long	When we're apart, I long for you.
Lovely	Your jet black hair is truly lovely.
Lust	My lust for you is unspeakable.
Magic	You bring magic into every moment we're together.
Meaningful	My life is meaningful since you came into it.

Nurture	You nurture my spirit.
Passion	I never knew passion until I met you.
Passionate	Our passionate evenings are unforgettable.
Pulchritude	You have both pulchritude and wit.
Radiance	Your radiance warms me.
Rapture	The rapture of your kiss sends me to new heights.
Romantic	Your romantic ways put a smile on my face.
Secure	I am secure in our love.
Sensuous	I desire your sensuous lips.
Sentimental	Your sentimental words touch my heart.
Serene	Your serene smile tells me you love me.
Sexy	I am consumed with thoughts of your sexy body.
Silken	Your silken hair feels like water falling on my face.
Smolder	A love that smolders must soon ignite.
Smooth	Your smooth skin drives me wild.
Soft	Your soft touch tames me.
Soul	My soul is one with yours.
Sparks	I see sparks when we embrace.
Sparkling	The sparkling of your eyes is like stars on a clear night.
Supple	Your supple body is tantalizing.
Tantalizing	Your tantalizing body is supple.
Tender	I love your tender words in the night.
Tingle	I tingle all over when I think of you.
Touch	Your touch is too much!
Tranquil	My heart is tranquil knowing we have each other.
Treasure	I treasure our weekends together.
Trusting	Your trusting way gives me security in our love.
Vital	You are the vital piece to the puzzle of my life.
Wanting	I am wanting for nothing now that you are in my life.
Warm	I look forward to your warm embrace.
Woo	I wuv you so I woo you.

Notes

Addresses

When Romeo Wrote Juliet

Your inspirational guide to the art of writing love letters

If you would like another copy of this book for yourself or someone close to you, please send a check or money order to:

> Stylus Publishing
> Dept R-10
> P.O. Box 2741
> Sunnyvale, CA 94087-0741

Price: ____ copies at $15.95 per copy   _____

Sales Tax: California residents please add 8.25% ($1.30) per book   _____

Shipping: Book rate (may take 3-4 weeks) is $2.00 for the first book and 75 cents for each additional book. Air Mail is $3.50 per book.   _____

                                        Total   _____

Ship to:

Name:_____

Street:_____

City:_____ State:_____ Zip:_____

Stylus Publishing

(408) 244-6344 Tel • (408) 244-6659 Fax